INTO THE BEAR PIT

INTO THE BEAR PIT

Mark James
with Martin Hardy

Virgin

This edition first published
in Great Britain in 2001 by
Virgin Publishing Ltd
Thames Wharf Studios
Rainville Road
London W6 9HA

First published in Great Britain in 2000

A catalogue record for the book is
available from the British Library.

ISBN 0 7535 0538 X

Typeset by TW Typesetting, Plymouth,
Devon

Printed and bound in Great Britain by
Mackays of Chatham PLC, Kent

Contents

Foreword

A few years ago, Suzanne and I found ourselves driving back from Scotland and decided to drop in on Mark and Jane in Yorkshire. We were not expecting to be fed, but Jesse offered and we were happy to accept his hospitality.

Jane is a wonderful cook, but she was out this day and it was Jesse who disappeared into the kitchen. About an hour later he re-emerged with a banquet . . . of Marmite sandwiches, a delicacy my liking of which borders on hatred. I'm the guy from the advertisement who takes a bite out of one, spits it out and runs off. Jane was livid when she discovered what he gave us because, unbeknown to him, there was a full ham and a cooked turkey in the cellar. It was the best meal we never had and I've never let Jesse forget.

At least it did not affect our friendship, which is as strong today as it was then. We first met at the Moroccan Open in the late seventies and we got on well straight away. It was not long before Jane also became a dear friend and our ties have never withered during two decades, five Ryder Cups as playing colleagues and the epic 1999 tussle in Boston when I was immensely proud to act as assistant – along with Ken Brown – to Jesse's captaincy.

I have always regarded Jesse as the strongest-minded player out there with a wonderful head on his shoulders. He deserved a far better partner than he got in the morning foursomes of the match at The Belfry in 1993 when I was injured and had to have a toenail removed that evening. I was so disappointed because he was playing great and I was simply horrible – no use to him whatsoever. When you play with a friend in the Ryder Cup you really want to be at your best.

Thankfully, we have had many good times together before and since, even though Jesse occasionally gives the impression that he is not enjoying himself. You should never judge a book by its cover because he has a great, dry sense of humour and is always fun to be around.

Jesse was not all that great company in the last round of the English Open in 1990 when we were in the last group. He was in one of his usual, head-down moods and hit a couple of shots on the run. As we came off the twelfth tee, I walked up alongside and said: 'What the hell's wrong with you? You're one shot out of second place, isn't that good enough for you? Get your finger out'. Of course, he then beat me in a play-off.

The measure of the man surfaced in 1998, however, when he actually asked me if I minded if he accepted the Ryder Cup captaincy. It was a typically warm gesture and, of course, I did not mind, actually encouraging him to do it because I was convinced I had one more match in me.

As it transpired I was injured for six months and Jesse nearly made it, but he was the right man to be captain. He did a great job in every respect; wonderful with every player and there was not a moment he would not spare for anyone. He looked after Ken and I as if we were kings and made our jobs so much easier than they could have been.

It was a strange experience for me because my job was totally different to anything I had come across in the Ryder Cup before. Watching as an assistant was totally different to spectating when still a member of the team. I did not feel as negative because when you are in the team and not selected for a particular series, your heart is always in your mouth, but as a vice captain I had so much confidence in the people I was watching.

I enjoyed everything about the experience. The team camaraderie was fantastic, as good as I have ever known it, although it is never worse than good in the European camp.

The only contentious issue, although it was never one inside the team room, concerned the three players who did not appear until the Sunday. I stood right behind Mark in what he decided. No disrespect to our lads, but I didn't believe we were as strong nine through twelve as the Americans were. It gave them greater options. They could put out their twelve fairly confidently whereas on Friday and Saturday we had to put out our best team and get as many points as we could.

Jesse got us a four-point lead on Saturday night and that's the captain's job done. What else can you say because the singles take care of themselves.

It was twelve against twelve and you just pray they do the best they can. For the first two days the teams Jesse put out were magnificent. Forget all this nonsense about tiredness because I've played all five series a couple of times and never even considered the thought of being tired. It's the Ryder Cup and if you can't get up for it you shouldn't be there. All right, on Sunday night you collapse, but by then it's all over.

Now it's my turn to be captain and I have no set plans for what I will do, but I do know I totally agreed with everything Jesse did in Boston. I'm so proud for myself and my family, and for my mum and dad. The Belfry could not be a better setting because of all the wonderful memories I have of the place.

I definitely benefited from serving under Jesse and I hope Suzanne and I can do as great a job as he and Jane did.

It was an honour for me to assist Jesse at Brookline, just as it is to contribute the foreword to *Into the Bear Pit*. He owes me nothing in return, but I do ask one favour. Qualify for my team, Mark.

Sam Torrance

Preface

The first time I ever thought about writing about my Ryder Cup history in general and what happened at Brookline in particular, was when Chubby Chandler, head of the rapidly expanding International Sports Management company, mentioned there might be a few bob in it. My ears pricked up and I started listening.

Once the idea of a book was put into my head and after I decided to do it, I saw the chance to address a few issues – not just relating to what happened in Boston but also to experiences through the years, particularly at the 1979 Ryder Cup when I was eventually fined a record amount by the golf authorities for offences I did not commit. I had never given my side of the story previously and considered, after twenty years, that it was about time it was aired. Murderers do not always get that length of sentence, so it seemed a suitable length of time had elapsed for me to offer the alternative view.

There were other considerations for putting pen to paper, not least the attitude of one or two American players during the match in Brookline. Their belief that there was nothing wrong did not tally with mine. I felt strongly that there was something amiss and that I should try to put it right for the future of what has become one of the greatest events in golf and, arguably, the biggest.

It is essential that we keep the game – and that is exactly what it is – high in the public esteem. Previous standards of sportsmanship and etiquette had placed it at the head of all sports and it has been rightly respected around the world. As a Ryder Cup captain, I considered I had a duty to try to restore an image which took a bit of a battering in Boston.

A book also gave me the chance to pay tribute to a wonderful woman – my wife Jane. I have always felt it was a two-person job and I would not have agreed to be captain if Jane had not accepted the chance to do the same for the ladies. I am pleased that she did accept and I think she did the job superbly. Jane more than pulled her weight while doing a tremendous job and she enabled me to concentrate 100 per cent on what I had to do. Jane has been an enormous influence and help throughout my career and I cannot thank her enough for all her support, not just in Brookline, but in all our time together.

My thanks to Martin Hardy for translating my ramblings into print.

The baton has now been passed on to Sam Torrance, a friend and colleague who was a wonderful assistant and, I am sure, will become a great captain.

To Jane, Sam, a magnificent team, and everybody else who has helped throughout my life, career and captaincy, many heartfelt thanks.

1 Rebel with a Cause

I T WAS ONLY WHEN THE BEDROOM began to fill with smoke, and the piercing wail of police sirens and fire engines grew louder, that I started to wonder whether things were going entirely to plan.

The scheme had been simple in its conception, design and, for half an hour or so, execution. It was back in the late 1970s, at the end of a long and painful season on the greens of the fast-developing European Tour. No end of rogue putters, none of which could be bent to the will of its master, had been in and out of the bag, but this latest B61 had brought me to a point where I was having a serious sense of humour failure. There was nothing wrong with the club – indeed, it was a very good club – but there came a time when I would always take out my frustration on that particular member of the family of fourteen.

The problem was almost certainly the puttee, not the putter, but one three-putt too many convinced me that, like many of its predecessors – and there had been plenty – it would have to go. It had misbehaved for the umpteenth time that year, and I was determined to make it suffer. It would be a slow and painful death, and I would enjoy every minute of it.

I was not quite sure what form the execution would take until I returned to my hotel room in Barcelona after the last round of the season. My temper at the time could best be described as steaming. Unable to get home that evening, I had time as well as the putter to kill. It was then that I saw the perfect answer to my quandary. There, in the corner of this grand room, with its high ceilings, elegant furniture and pleasant paintings, was a fireplace. The offending weapon would be a burnt sacrifice to the golfing gods. Wonderful.

Slowly, carefully, and with no little relish, I began to collect every single inflammable item in the room belonging to me or my room-mate, Ken Brown, who played a big part in my sporting life and Ryder Cup career, then and to this day. After all the torture it had given me, I was absolutely determined to make the putter endure a particularly painful death, so I stood it up next to the fireplace so that it could watch me setting up this wonderful fire. Old golf-ball boxes, tournament information sheets, room-service menus, newspapers, carrier bags, scorecards, yardage books, even old golf gloves were arranged in the grate. There were plenty of those because Ken used to get through at least four a round in those days, and probably cost Titleist a fortune. I thought the thin leather would prove a longer-lasting source of fuel.

Finally, I stuck the grip end of the putter up the chimney and rested the other end on the pile of material. I then found some matches, and soon we had ignition. The fire took hold quickly, and I remember thinking just how intense the heat was. I basked in its glow. It was simply beautiful.

There was some lead tape on the back of the putter, and watching it bubble and drip away gave me a great deal of pleasure. The rubber at the top of the grip soon began to turn black and smoulder. At one point it was almost as if it was screaming in pain. Oh, the joy of it! I have never felt so much pleasure; it was pure delight. I could not have imagined a better end for this objectionable article. It had done the dirty on me for so long, and now it was payback time.

The fire was going well, the papers burning with rich, bright colours, and I lay on my stomach on the bed gazing deeply into this small but majestic inferno. I could not remember when I had had such a damn good time. Suddenly, the whole thing started to smoke quite heavily as the glove leather took hold, and great clouds came puffing back into the room. The chimney, it turned out, was blocked not too far above the fireplace, and it was too late to do anything about it. I had ignored the blowback initially because there was only a little smoke, but now it began to fill the room. All of a sudden we had the beginnings of a major incident on our hands.

I opened the door and window to get a bit of a through-draft going but, typical of my luck at the time, it proved the wrong thing to do. The draft blew all the smoke into the hotel rather than out of the window, and set off the alarms. Ten minutes later we had fire engines and police descending on the hotel, and the manager was hot-footing it towards our room. He was not happy. He may or may not have been called Basil – or, as we were in Spain, Manuel – but it certainly must have looked like a scene from *Fawlty Towers*.

Ken and I, of course, knowing exactly the source of all the smoke, did not respond to the alarms or the calls to evacuate the hotel. We were resting on the bed, listening to all the sirens and the shouting on the streets outside and waiting for the fire to die along with the putter, when the manager finally stormed into the room. All he could splutter was: 'Is no possible to light fire here. No possible!' I replied, 'It is possible, because I did it a few minutes ago.' 'Is no possible!' he continued, but I was adamant. 'Yes it is. I've just done it, and it was great.'

The fire eventually petered out, the alarms stopped and the police and firemen disappeared. They actually allowed us to remain in the hotel, although they sent a bill for £1,500 to our travel agent to pass on. I refused to pay. If there is a fireplace in your room, I firmly maintain you should be allowed to light a fire in it.

The episode was a classic example of the kinds of things that were happening to us during that period. It was incredible how often Ken, my partner in all things which went wrong in those days, and I landed in trouble without really trying – and in many respects deserving to. It was uncanny.

Ken and I had arrived together on tour with no expectations and had quickly hooked up, both of us young at a time when there were few young players around. We were treated with apprehension, although a few players were more welcoming than others. I remember Neil Coles, Eddie Polland, Malcolm Gregson and Harry Bannerman being tremendously helpful. They always gave of their time and welcomed us on tour, but some of the others appeared not to want young players coming through. Maybe they wanted more respect than we were prepared to give, at least until we knew them. There was almost certainly an element of that. In those days most players did not put in an awful lot of time on the range and putting green, but Ken and I were always there together and enjoyed each other's company – a situation which exists to this day. We were room-mates and soul-mates, and, if the authorities could have had their way in the forthcoming years, cell-mates too. Trouble seemed to be our middle name.

Ken's game was built on a low, weak slice off the tee using an ugly, laminated wooden driver with a picture of Zebedee on the top (his long game would improve rapidly over the years though, until he was one of our finest strikers), but he had a fantastic short game and was the best course manager I had ever seen. I was a pretty poor player, wild and rough round the edges, so although I knew of the Ryder Cup, it was not something which occupied too much of my thinking. When you turn professional you do not have specific ambitions; equally, there are no restrictions. Golf was just something I liked doing, and wanted to do as a career. It was as simple as that for me.

My only target when I first became a golfing gypsy was to be as good as I could be. I got a hint of how good that might be when I finished fifth in Johnny Miller's Open at Royal Birkdale in 1976 after shooting a final-round 66. This was followed by a second place in the Benson and Hedges a few weeks later, and suddenly I realised that in spite of one or two splutters along the way, I was not out of my depth. Having arrived without any preconceived notions, I was delighted to finish fifteenth on the money list and be voted the tour's rookie of the year.

Now that I knew I could compete to a certain extent, my personal target became the 1977 Ryder Cup team, the last time Great Britain and Ireland tackled the Americans without the help of the rest of Europe. My play in the build-up to the match at Royal Lytham and St Anne's was not particularly impressive, but after collecting £5,100 and as many points as I could by the cut-off stage, I was eleventh on the standings and was handed a wild card place. What made it all the more pleasing was that Ken also made the team.

The number of matches had been cut from the normal 32 to just 20, the theory being that it might give us a better chance. Some suspected it was a damage limitation exercise. Whatever the reason, there were five foursomes on the first day, five fourballs on the second and ten singles on the last. It was simply a case of our seeing how well we could do and their knowing that they would almost certainly win; when the Great

Britain and Ireland team halved in 1969 at Royal Birkdale it was considered an incredible result, and the last victory had been in 1957 at Lindrick. In between, the matches were one-sided. We had never had great teams and, to be honest, not many good players either. Nick Faldo came into that 1977 team alongside Ken and me, and he was obviously en route to becoming a very good player. He looked to have the class and the short game, everything necessary to do well, together with the ability to play well under the most severe pressure. He was paired with Peter Oosterhuis, who had been European number one four years in succession in the early 1970s, and that certainly made a strong partnership. But apart from Faldo, Oosterhuis, Tony Jacklin, Neil Coles, Eamonn Darcy and Brian Barnes, there were few decent players. To be perfectly honest, the rest of us were not that good.

Compared to America, European golf was only just getting going. Qualifying School did not start until 1976; when I had turned professional a year earlier, you had to go six months before you were allowed to keep any prize money. Most players came on tour as club assistants, selling tee pegs one minute and teeing it up against one another the next, and you had to do between three and five years with a club before you could set foot on tour. It was not a situation conducive to grooming world-class players. The rules started to relax in 1976 though, and people started to come on tour in bigger numbers. More good players began to come through, and we started moving towards the situation we have today, with talent flooding in from tributaries throughout the world.

Until the balance of power started to tilt in the 1980s, making a Ryder Cup team was not something Americans particularly set their sights on. If they made it, it was generally a case of, 'OK, we'll have a trip over to little ol' England, spank the bottom of the British and Irish players, do a bit of shopping, see a sight or two, take in a few ruins and come home with the cup.' That is how it happened most of the time, and it only changed in 1983, four years after Europe was allied to the Great Britain and Ireland team. That one-point defeat at Palm Beach Gardens, Florida, was the first sign of the golden years to follow.

Our captain for the 1977 competition, Brian Huggett, was a no-nonsense guy who told it as it was. For the first day's foursomes he decided, in his wisdom, to send me out last, alongside Tommy Horton. 'On the tee, representing the United States of America, Jack Nicklaus and Tom Watson.' It has to be said, there was a considerable gulf in terms of ability and performance between the two partnerships. Jack and Tom were pretty much at their peak; Tommy and I were facing the two best players in the world, who a few months earlier had gone head to head at the Open at Turnberry in one of the most memorable shoot-outs in the sport's history. Nicklaus was such a good player then that if he hit a fade it moved about four feet left to right; if he hit a wild slice it moved twelve feet in the same direction. Watson was nearly as powerful as his partner, and I had never seen anyone with chipping ability quite like his. I got the impression with Nicklaus and Watson that they knew how good they were, although not in a boastful way. I have played with both of them a number of times since – times when they have shot big numbers as well as low – and they have never been anything less than absolute gentlemen and great fun to play with, but they knew that unless they had a really off day, there was no way we could play well enough to beat them.

That first occasion for me was more of an experience than a pleasure, although I do not remember suffering from any nerves. It has to be admitted that we got all the breaks that day, otherwise it could have been really one-sided. We lost 5 & 4, and did extremely well to make it last that long. After three or four holes, I remember thinking: 'These guys are fantastically good.' Even among the top players they really were majestic, and they made me realise one thing: there would be every chance I was never going to be as good as them.

The next day I was pleased to be paired with Ken in the fourballs against Hale Irwin and Lou Graham – not quite as daunting a task, but still a formidable partnership. It was a much better match for me. They did not play that well, we ham-and-egged reasonably adequately and made a game of it. There is a clip from this game shown quite often on television when they replay old Ryder Cup footage, of Browny almost chipping in at the last from the back edge to a front pin, a little bump-and-run shot which stopped on the lip of the hole. We lost one down.

I do not remember too much about the singles, although I lost 2 & 1 to Ray Floyd, a very good player who could always get the most out of his game. It is a talent many guys have now, but not many had it then. Floyd was never a classical swinger or great striker, but he worked the ball round brilliantly.

And that was my introduction to the Ryder Cup. It was a lot more relaxed in those days, with few rules and restrictions. There were few people around too, and you could go down the street or wander around the course without interruption. There was no team room as such, and nobody batted an eyelid if you went out for an evening. Indeed, Ken, Eamonn Darcy – who was starting to make a big name for himself – and I went out to a night club in Blackpool one night. No one kept tabs on us at all, not that we would have messed with captain Huggett had there been a curfew of any sort: he was not nicknamed the British Bulldog for nothing. I do not remember being late back in – it was probably about one o'clock; when you are that age you can get away with a couple of nights without sleep, and neither Ken nor I drank. There was absolutely no question of us staggering back in the middle of the night, we were totally sober and going out was just a natural thing to do, but twenty years on, just think what the headline writers would make of Ryder Cup players spotted in a night club during competition, even if they were sober.

We were not getting into trouble at that stage, but this situation was quickly rectified. It did not bother us if people took a dislike to us because we had a don't-give-a-damn attitude which was fairly evident in some of our behaviour. I first fell foul of officialdom in the early part of 1977. I had a nasty shock when I was fined £50 for pulling out of the Portuguese Open: I had a bad knee and could not get a caddie. That really rankled, because I had played the first round at Penina and shot 75 over a relatively flat course. The next round was at Palmares, a very hilly course. There were no caddies, and I would have had to pull my own trolley – a physical impossibility given my dodgy knee. Only a matter of minutes before my start time, I informed them I would not be turning up. The fine was incomprehensible to me, and a very clear indication of the way the committee regarded the younger players. I really got a feeling we were never going to get a fair crack of the whip from some of the elder statesmen on tour. Some of them were never going to like us whatever we did.

I never saw myself as a rebel. I could throw a club and look downcast, something for which I would get a bit of stick in the press, but I had never done anything you might term 'rebellious'. I was just like a lot of young players: slightly out of control on the course, but nothing serious. Nobody would turn a hair these days. There was never a question of my having a chip on my shoulder because I never had anything to have a chip about. I just wanted to go out and play golf and see how I performed. The problem stemmed, almost certainly as I have said, from the fact that Ken and I never gave anyone respect without knowing them first. We treated people, whoever they were, as we found them; if they were nice and friendly, then we showed respect, even if we had never heard of them. I do not really know if that is the right or wrong way to go about things, but it was definitely how we felt. We were out to make our way in the world and we treated people according to their personalities, not what they had achieved or how they wanted to be treated. If we came into contact with people who felt they deserved more instant respect from us, then there were likely to be problems.

That £50 fine did not sour me completely, but the experience made me wary of the hierarchy in general and the way things worked, that things could at times seem hugely unfair. The fine was not a monumental figure, but it was the principle. I really could not understand why they imposed it. To get fined when you feel you have done nothing wrong hurts. I paid up, grudgingly. I do not forget about things like that, and from that point on I started to get into more trouble with the powers-that-be. Had anybody said in 1977 that I would one day be the Ryder Cup captain, I would have immediately insisted on their committal to the nearest asylum.

My reputation as a rebel gained momentum (not by design), and Zambia in 1978 proved to be a real problem spot. The top twenty finishers in those days had to turn up for the prize-giving ceremony, and I had finished third. The ceremony was due to take something ridiculous like an hour and a half to complete. I still had my floppy hat on from playing when I walked up to collect my envelope, then moving to one side together with the other players. I tore the top off the envelope and held it up to look into it. I started shaking it, but of course nothing fell out because there was never anything in there to start with. I was warming to my task by this time and really started to shake this envelope up and down, but to no avail. It was a little bit distracting because some of the crowd were chuckling, but it was fairly amusing, especially if you have an IQ like mine – low.

Anyway, I soon received a letter from the Zambian golfing authorities informing me that I was being fined £250 for slouching around during the presentation ceremony and wearing an offensive hat. I found that last charge particularly hard to accept because I had been given the hat out there. It had AFRI-COCO written on it, so perhaps that had some sort of negative connotation in Zambia. And that was not the end of the eating into my prize money: I was also fined for throwing a club. It did not hit anybody, but it did smack against a tree which dislodged some fruit which hit a spectator on the head – another example of how my luck was starting to change, and not for the better.

By the 1978 Italian Open – which would turn into one of my finest hours as a so-called 'rebel' – I was getting particularly browned off. I hurt my wrist, which was not particularly difficult to do because the Pevero course was mainly rock with a small amount of grass between tees and greens, and after ten holes it was aching so much I could not risk injuring it further. But there was no way I could pull out. The last time I had done that through injury I had been fined. A precedent had been set, so I had to come up with an alternative plan, and I did: I would play the last ten holes one-handed. It must have been distracting for my playing partners, but it did not really occur to me then. I shot 111, and the press just loved it. I gave them plenty of quotes to go with their stories, reminding them that I had been fined £50 the last time I had pulled out injured, so this time I had thought I had better carry on.

I was summoned to appear before the committee, and was asked exactly what I thought I was playing at. 'Golf' did not seem an appropriate answer in the circumstances, so I told them exactly what I felt, and that if they had a problem with it just to let me know what they wanted me to do in terms of withdrawing or not when injured. My solicitors would have been on the case if they had fined me because I would not have paid it, but they only reprimanded me this time. They did not like it though, because I was challenging their authority, but all I was doing was standing up for myself and telling them that what they had done to me the previous year was wrong. They were not best pleased by this effrontery.

They were in a similar state of mind when Ken and I got to the Ryder Cup in Greenbrier in 1979. There was a tangible feeling that they were determined to keep an eye on us. And didn't they just.

2 *Star Trek* Time

I F I WAS ATTRACTING A FEW VIGOROUS head-shakes from the establishment, Ken Brown was also showing some traits that would raise a few eyebrows and temperatures along the corridors of European Tour power. My good friend was being fined virtually every month for slow play – something which might have baffled him, but few of those who played with him were surprised: when Ken putted you could see the grass grow under his feet. He was diabolically slow. When he stood over a putt you were never sure which would come first: his backstroke or darkness.

Nothing much had happened to me on the disciplinary front in the rest of 1978, or in the run-up to the Greenbrier in 1979, although I was fined the odd time for throwing a club. I had no problem coughing up if it was justified, and I got my just deserts in this respect at the Welsh Classic at Wenvoe, a tournament I was to go on and win, when I speared a club into the green. I was actually trying to launch it over the ropes and into the trees, but unfortunately I hung on to it, and as the club sank into the soft turf I got that sinking feeling that attacks your nervous system when you do something which makes you look a complete prat. I repaired the damage and paid the £20 fine without a quibble.

Certain players still made it clear they did not like me, but that did not bother me at all. Actually, I quite enjoyed it. If somebody dislikes you, you can always steer clear of him. Ken had similar feelings, and by this time we were both doing pretty well as golfers, much to the displeasure of the authorities – but who gave a damn? We certainly did not. I had won the European Match Play in 1978, then followed my Welsh Classic triumph in 1979 with the Irish Open. I was inside the top ten in the money list the first year, and finished third the year after, and I made the Ryder Cup team automatically, which was a great thrill. I felt by now I was one of the better players, and actually belonged on tour. It was also satisfying to see Ken in the team, although amazingly it would prove to be our last Ryder Cup together. Looking back, maybe that was not such a bad thing, but at the time if somebody had said, 'You two will not make the same team again,' we would have curled up laughing.

The organisation of the competition was nowhere near as thorough as it is today. There was no team get-together at a hotel before; we just turned up at Heathrow to check in, whereupon we were invariably handed boarding cards for economy class, whereas today only the pointy end of the plane will suffice. I was living in Stamford, Lincolnshire, at the time and it had never taken me more than an hour and a half to get to the airport. This occasion would prove the exception to that rule. A succession of traffic jams down the A1 meant my arrival was delayed. I got there in plenty of time to catch the flight, but I was missing when everybody else was milling around beforehand. It was just one of those unfortunate things, but indicative of the rotten luck which was to dog me all week. This incident also turned out to be one of the many things held against Ken and me when we came back.

Contrary to popular belief about my state of dress when I finally walked under the WELCOME TO HEATHROW sign, I did have the team uniform on in all its glory, although I can think of other words to describe it. In those days, most of what we were expected to wear looked as if it was meant for somebody either five times bigger or shorter. I cannot remember if we had a fitting for this get-up, but probably not. The only item I was wearing which did not conform to the official outfit was a pair of suede shoes, and I was only wearing those because I did not want to risk blistering my feet on the drive down or walking through airports. The leather ones we had been given were uncomfortable, but I did have them in my carry-on luggage just in case we had a team photograph taken. Maybe I was not 100 per cent team uniform, but if there was a problem I made sure I was in a position quickly to rectify it.

If not wearing the correct shoes got me off on the wrong foot, so to speak, then things quickly deteriorated as soon as we reached the USA. I tore a rib cartilage taking my luggage off the carousel. It was not only very painful, but restricted me to such an extent that, despite cortisone injections, I played just the first morning and then took no further part in the match.

If the shoes and the rib had been the only problems on that trip it would not have been so bad, but when things went wrong for Ken and me in those days, they went spectacularly wrong. I imagine some people, especially those who were keeping their beady eyes on us, might have considered my injury a bit of a fake, because between arrival and the first round things went seriously pear-shaped. The welcome dinner went reasonably well, but the gala dinner was not good. In fact, it could not have been much worse. I had a splitting headache, and we were all seated up and down a fifty-yard-long table, high on a platform. The teams and the officials were looking out over the throng, and for some unknown reason they trained quite powerful spotlights on us all. If there was anything likely to make my headache worse, bright lights would definitely do the trick. They did.

I forced down the main course, and then said, 'I want to leave.' I cannot remember the exact words of the discussion that ensued, but I remember officialdom not being best pleased. In fact, it was not pleased at all, but when your head is banging the last thing you need is noise and bright lights. It was a nightmare – one more black mark in a black book which was already several pages long.

Come the opening ceremony, things began to go downhill so fast we needed skis. The ceremony was scheduled for 4.30 p.m. in a sports hall 400 yards from our hotel. Ken and I were never heavily into personal grooming, and we never needed long to change; we worked out that half an hour would be more than enough to dress and head off for the hall. That was the plan, but it did not work out like that, which was hardly surprising considering our luck was in serious freefall.

We were practising on the afternoon of the ceremony, chipping away with our Ryder Cup jumpers tied round our waists. Ken was wearing a floppy hat and looked as if he weighed about four stone. We headed back to the hotel at half-past three and Ken decided to go for a haircut, which was odd, because neither of us had ever been encumbered by anything even approaching a hairstyle. Still, I said, 'I'll give you a knock at ten past four and we'll wander down to the opening.' When I left Ken, it was 3.40 p.m.

When I went into my room the first thing I saw was a piece of paper which had been pushed under the door. It read: 'Team meeting, 3.45'. Oh no! I rushed down to find Ken, who was by now covered in towels and in the middle of a trim, and grabbed him. The meeting room took some finding, but it was only just after quarter to four when we walked in – the only people in golf attire. The other players and officials were in suits. The feeling we had in our stomachs was not an uncommon one. They looked at us as if we were aliens, and said, 'What on earth are you doing?' We told the truth, and said, 'We've just got back from the course, discovered there was a team meeting and came straight here.' Our captain, John Jacobs, replied, 'Well you're supposed to be here in your suits, so go and get changed.' John was one of the few in the party I did have time for, but we could sense there was general disapproval. Indeed, had some of their heads shaken any more, things might have started to fall out. We could tell some of the senior players thought we were taking the mickey, when actually nothing could have been further from the truth. All we were doing was trying to get through the day, and failing.

Ken and I immediately headed back to our adjacent rooms, and within minutes there was a knock on the door. It was five minutes past four, and Tommy Horton was standing there saying, 'Are you ready?' I replied, 'No. We've still got twenty-five minutes.' I was getting annoyed. They kept on badgering us, saying they would send a car to pick us up. They kept on and on, and we were in that car before a quarter past four for what was only about a half a minute's ride. We were seriously pissed off. We could have played another hole.

On the list of misdemeanours it appeared as being late for a team meeting and for the opening ceremony. Then we were accused of yawning and fidgeting during the national anthem. There was a definite feeling that we were being frowned upon, and we were less than enamoured with the way we were being treated.

Thank heavens the match was about to start. Ken and I were paired against Fuzzy Zoeller and Lee Trevino, and I was sure I would be all right. Once again I was wrong: we lost, and I was in absolute agony and could not play again. It was a nightmare because I was desperate to get out there and play. I do not know if any of the others felt I had had enough and just did not want to play, but that certainly was not the case. I spent the rest of the match on a buggy with John Jacobs. We seemed to get on fine, and two years later he gave me a wild card, so he could not have held any grudges. Anyway, the problem was not with John, but with some of the other players and officials.

Things went relatively well for the rest of the weekend. Let's face it, they had to improve. Wrong again. The official dinner saw me sitting next to Sandy Lyle. Sandy was a wonderful golfer, but his patience level at official functions was not terribly high. At the end of the meal, by which time we were all losing the will to live, Sandy was rolling up petits fours, putting them on the edge of his spoon and flicking them at the American officials. It has to be said he was a damn good shot, but guess who got the blame? It went straight on to my list of misdemeanours, but here the truth comes out. It was Sandy. He had had half a shandy too much.

And there was another transgression, one I am not proud of. We were signing menus at the gala dinner, and for some obscure reason I put (s.o.b.) after Sandy's name. It was not a reflection on Sandy because we're great mates, but it certainly deserved a slap round the head. The menu apparently belonged to a vicar, and that did not help my case one little bit. It was not a very clever thing to do. If I deserved to be fined for anything, it was that. It was proof that I could be stupid if I put my mind to it.

And that still is not the end of the story. We got to the check-out the next morning, and another team member, Michael King, known to everybody as Queenie, said to me, 'Where's your suitcase?' I said, as a joke, 'I've thrown the lot away. None of it fitted, so

I've ditched it.' In fact, I had already checked in. I have often wondered over the years if anyone else has ever been accused by the authorities of throwing away his own clothes when he no longer needed them. In my case, it was another item for the list. I found that quite remarkable. I arrived home and did not think I was in any trouble. Wrong.

Many things have been written about what happened that week, much of it totally fictitious. It was said, for instance, that Brian Barnes nearly thumped me. I was at an age when I would not have been the least bit bothered if he had. He would probably have knocked me out, but I would have come round, got an eight iron and crept up on him. It was all rubbish. I would definitely remember if Barnesy had threatened to hit me. Bernard Gallacher's wife Lesley told me years later that at one stage she took me to one side and gave me a damn good talking to. If she remembers that, then I am prepared to go along with her story, but I have no recollection of it. It was even said that John Jacobs had threatened to send me home. That was simply not the case. Why the press needed to resort to fiction I do not know. The truth was strange enough.

Ken and I were indelibly labelled rebels, bad guys, whatever, and it was a title neither of us felt we deserved. Several weeks after we returned from the USA, at Woburn for the Dunlop Masters, we were summoned to appear in front of the committee. We were told to be there at five o'clock, and we were there at the appointed hour. At twenty minutes to six we still had not been called. Barnesy was probably up for something, but whatever the reason we were left waiting, twiddling our putters. I was a big *Star Trek* fan at the time, still am, and an episode was on that evening. If I did not go home straight away (Stamford is one hour and 25 minutes' drive from Woburn) I was in danger of missing it, so I said to Ken, 'I'm off. *Star Trek*'s on at ten past seven.' I was not going to miss it for anybody. I thought they would understand.

Ken went into the meeting alone, expecting about ten people. But this match had pulled in a record attendance for a committee meeting: there were 25 tour officials and committee members in there, including Lord Derby, the then president of the PGA. There was an empty chair at one end of the table with a light over it. Ken told them what I had said about *Star Trek*, and some of them were livid. They obviously did not have a sense of humour, but Neil Coles was laughing so uncontrollably he could hardly sit up. They had no choice but to go through the misdemeanours as planned, a list about three feet long, in the main compiled by Tommy Horton and Bernard Gallacher.

The next summons was for the December meeting in London. Fortunately there was no *Star Trek* on that night, so I headed off towards the capital. I was a client of Mark McCormack's International Management Group at the time, and I was told by John Simpson, who looked after my interests, that if I kicked up a fuss there was every likelihood I would not be invited to the following year's US Masters. I faced the committee, said 'Not true' to about nineteen charges and 'True' to the (s.o.b.) on the menu. They were absolutely convinced I had transgressed left, right and centre; I was just as convinced they were going to hammer me. I was not disappointed. They were going to fine me no matter what, and they did, creating a new record at the same time. I broke the previous UK all-comers' best by a mile and a half: they took away my match fee of £1,000 and fined me an extra £500 on top – one twentieth of my annual takings then and equivalent to £50,000 today if you finished in the same position on the money list. That sort of money could have fuelled the *Starship*

Enterprise for a couple of trips round the galaxy. I felt I had been treated badly, although some obviously believed I got exactly what I deserved, and I vowed to stay away from the people responsible for inflicting this great injustice. I did not want anything to do with them, it was as simple as that.

The mammoth fine soured things for me to a certain extent, but I did not get into any more trouble in the next two years as the maturing process started to kick in. Of greater significance during that period was my meeting and marrying Jane, a pretty, intelligent girl who tells it as it is. Her influence started giving me a different slant on my actions, and it was because of her that I gradually started to clean up my act and generally tried to behave a lot better. I learnt that sometimes it can be better to back away from confrontation.

One head-to-head I had little chance of avoiding during the time Ken and I kept finding ourselves in trouble came when the two of us were sharing a car in the USA. I suddenly became aware of a police car parked ahead and eased off the accelerator to make our speed a little more respectable. Unfortunately, as we passed the highway patrolman, Ken took it upon himself to make a rude gesture from the passenger seat. A couple of minutes later we were pulled over, ordered out of the car and told to put our hands on the bonnet and spread our legs. It came as a great relief when I discovered the officer only wanted to frisk us, although he did make it quite clear what would happen if there was a repeat performance. It has to be admitted that although we believed we were being blighted by bad luck, we did occasionally bring it upon ourselves.

Come 1982 I had been a professional on the road for about six years, and I felt a lot better about myself, the tour and life in general. It was time to take a quantum leap: I joined the committee. The irony of my decision was not lost on me, just as it was not when the time came to accept the Ryder Cup captaincy. Those kinds of ironies in life appeal to my sense of humour. There were two reasons for the one-time rebel to join what many considered to be the establishment. Firstly, the opportunity presented itself; secondly, there were more and more players like me appearing on the tour, and the make-up of the committee at that time bore no resemblance to the rest of us. There was no way things would change just by having people on the outside bitching. The only way to progress was to get in there and try to change things. That is what I set out to do, and today, with the help of a lot of other players, we have a body representative of the players that is both positive and healthy. Everybody knows exactly what is going on, which was certainly not the case when I started out.

But even then, when I was slowly becoming part of the establishment that had been on my back ever since I started playing golf, if anyone had told me that in 1999 I would captain the Ryder Cup team in the USA, I would have laughed in his face.

3 Captain Material

T HE RYDER CUP CAPTAINCY was something I had neither sought nor thought about at all during my career until after the 1997 competition at Valderrama, during which I had helped Seve Ballesteros. After that historic first win on continental soil, and in the run-up to the December committee meeting that year, I spoke to Sam Torrance about who was going to be the next captain. We just about came to the same conclusion: there were not that many candidates apart from the two of us. It was going to be a tricky decision because neither of us had gone after the captaincy or discussed it in any detail with anybody. I was not particularly ambitious in that area, and I think Sam considered it as something which might come to him one day, but he was not interested in chasing it either. Both of us still had our playing careers to consider.

It was with these issues in mind that we went into the committee meeting where the matter would be discussed. I was chairman and Sam a member, and it was not a long debate. The decision reached was the same as Sam and I had reached privately: there were very few possibilities, and Sam and I were the leading contenders. Ken Brown's name was thrown into the hat too, but I knew he was never really that bothered. Peter Oosterhuis, Europe's finest in his day and a Ryder Cup stalwart, was known to be interested and he was also seriously considered, but the popular opinion seemed to be that Oosty had not been on tour for a long time, and although he was both popular and very highly respected, the time gap was perhaps too long. To take the job these days it is desirable for players and captain to know one another pretty well, because it makes it that much easier in the team room. This is a fairly recent innovation, because during the 1980s and earlier it did not matter that much because the team room was not such a private place; now it is considered essential to have a close bond between captain and players. That counted against Oosty, although I am sure he would have made a fine leader.

One or two other names were bandied about, but for the likes of the younger Bernhard Langer and Ian Woosnam it was considered they would be far too useful to the team in a playing capacity, although ultimately that would prove not to be the case as both failed to qualify. The playing aspect of the Ryder Cup was something Sam and I were still particularly interested in, so I persuaded the committee that because we were both active and wanted to make the next team, the best course of action would be to defer appointing a captain at least until June 1998. That way we could see who was or was not playing well, because we were both in our mid-forties – an age at which one's game can start to suffer. It does become slightly more difficult every year no matter what standard you have played to; the endless merry-go-round of airports, hotels and courses takes its toll after a couple of decades.

In the spring of the 1998 season I was playing like a haddock, while Sam's form was on an ever-increasing high. He was in a non-drinking phase at the time, which was certainly very disturbing for those who have known him through the years. It was not something his friends encouraged, but the decision seemed to be working in his favour, and in June he claimed the

French Open title to find himself in a situation where he could launch a prolonged campaign once qualification started in September. The powers-that-be approached me, but I told them I would have to speak to Sam first. I told him I would take the captaincy as long as he was not interested, because I did not want any bad feelings with someone who had been such a close friend and colleague over the years. Sam told me to go for it because he was still very keen to play. It was only then that I said I would love to accept the position, even though inside I knew I too wanted to be in the team rather than leading it.

I had had a sniff of what captaincy might be about at the 1980 Kirin Cup in Japan. The top six in the points list were eligible for this competition, but quite often the big boys did not play because they wanted vast amounts of appearance money. This happens now and again, but it is less prevalent now since the advent of players like Lee Westwood and Darren Clarke, who will play without receiving a briefcase loaded with cash as long as everybody else is treated the same. Back in the early 1980s, though, we had had to trawl through the lower ranks of the money list, and ended up with an extremely diverse team: me, Ireland's Ronan Rafferty, Scotland's Gordon Brand Jr, Sweden's Anders Forsbrand, Spain's José Rivero and Mark Mouland. The US Tour faxed us asking for a list of the players representing Europe, and after we replied they sent word back that they had requested a list of the players, not the caddies. We might have been a B team, but I was soon given an indication of what might be achieved with a bit of team spirit. We all got on marvellously, and only narrowly lost to a very powerful American side in the final.

Team spirit would be an important factor in my plans for the 1999 team, even though some would try to disrupt it from outside. Once the announcement of my appointment was made, it did not take long for Tony Jacklin to crawl out of the woodwork and air his views. It would not be the Ryder Cup if Tony Jacklin did not stick his oar in somewhere along the line, and on this occasion he did not disappoint us. I have never been able to understand why some people cannot leave centre stage and retire to the back benches with a little more grace. But Jacklin's criticism of my appointment, based principally on the Greenbrier episode twenty years earlier, did not bother me particularly. If he could verbally attack his successor and one-time friend Bernard Gallacher, then he would certainly not be hanging back when I took the job.

I knew I would get absolutely knocked to hell in some quarters when I accepted the captaincy, but I felt I could do it, that I knew the players well enough and was more than capable of handling whatever came with the territory. Criticism was what I expected, and it was so predictable it was almost unnerving. It is remarkable that one particular person can show such disapproval yet everyone seems unaffected by it on a personal level. What Jacklin failed to understand was that people change. You can be a bad player one year and a great one twenty years later; nobody says you do not deserve to win a major because once upon a time you could not hit the ball.

I was in two minds whether to respond to Jacklin's comments or shrug them off, so I sat down with Jane, Richard Hills (the Ryder Cup director) and Mitchell Platts (the tour's director of communications and public relations). They advised that I would be better off letting it go, and that is what I did. A response from me would have been like an open invitation to carry on with the debate, and that would have been the wrong thing to do.

I rarely hear people saying good things about Jacklin, and considering he had a fairly short but great career that is a shame. He took the Ryder Cup forward and upward, and there is no question he was instrumental in Europe's victories in 1985 at the Belfry and 1987, when we won for the first time on American soil. Unfortunately, he was never somebody I understood or warmed to, and the feeling was obviously mutual. It happens.

I was just fifteen when Jacklin won the Open at a time when Arnold Palmer and Jack Nicklaus were my heroes – real gentlemen on the course, no malice in either of them, which is always heartwarming in players who are that good. When I came on tour Jacklin was playing predominantly in the States, although I was aware of what he had done and that he and Peter Oosterhuis were our top players. It was a few years before I played with Jacklin for the first time, and by then he was on the wane. He had been a fantastic putter, but now it was leaving him, and I did not consider him as impressive a player as some who were around at the time, such as Eamonn Darcy. Darce was simply tremendous; I watched in awe as he practised. He would clip the ball away and it invariably went dead straight. He was a beautiful striker of the ball. Jacklin certainly did not stand comparison with him, but then it had been six years since he had won a major championship and I never really saw him in his golden period.

I remember little of Jacklin in the Ryder Cup team of 1977, but I was impressed by the way captain Brian Huggett dealt with one episode during my debut. There was less golf played in that match: one series of foursomes on the first day, another of fourballs on the second and just ten singles on the last. On one of the first two days there was a match still left out on the course and, quite rightly, everybody who had finished was expected to go along and support. I think Jacklin was in the clubhouse having tea and scones; he certainly was not out there with the rest of us, and Huggett fell out with him over that. As a result, the former Open champion on both sides of the Atlantic was left out of the last day's singles. It was a brave move to make, but there was no bullshit with Huggett. He had not approved of what one of his team had done, and he was determined to do something about it. Jacklin was similarly anonymous as far as I was concerned two years later at the Greenbrier, but from what he said when I was made captain he clearly remembers me, and was not best pleased with my behaviour.

I only played under Jacklin's captaincy once, at the Belfry in 1989, and I cannot say I was terribly impressed with his decision-making. It was Ronan Rafferty's only Ryder Cup, and I had said to the young Irishman at the start of the week that if he had any problems he did not want to bother Jacklin with, then he could have a word with me and we could discuss it. My offer was duly accepted after one of the practice rounds when I had been playing with my good friend Howard Clark. Jacklin had given Ronan to Bernhard Langer, but Ronan simply said, 'I can't play with Bernhard.'

Apparently, they had reached the tee at the par five fourth and Ronan, who had played wonderfully all year and ended up with three wins and first place in the Order of Merit, pulled out his driver. It seemed the sensible thing to do because few could remember the last time he had missed a fairway. Now Bernhard's game was totally different, and he wanted his four-somes partner to take a four iron off the tee to take the bunkers out of play. There was a thirty-yard gap between the traps and Ronan felt capable of hitting it, but Bernhard was leaving nothing to chance. His plan was a four iron followed by a three wood and then an eight iron to the green, but that was not the way Ronan saw it. Little instances like that, differences in game play, had convinced the Irishman their partnership could not work.

I figured Jacklin would want Ronan to play a good few matches because of the way he had been performing all season, so I spoke to the captain, telling him of Ronan's misgivings and suggesting that he could pair Ronan with Howard, which made sense because they both played the same ball. It was not that I did not want to play with Howard, just that Ronan was such a valuable player who ought to be used where it would benefit him and the team most. I knew Bernhard would not have a problem playing with me because he is a very good team man who will always play with anybody and give it 100 per cent. Jacklin had happily sent out Ronan with Langer on the first morning, whereupon they lost to Mark Calcavecchia and Ken Green, then he tried him with fellow Irishman Christy O'Connor Jr on the second day, but they too lost to the same American pair. Ronan gained his revenge on Calcavecchia in the singles, but he played just two series before the last day, including the one with Langer, and that seemed a surprising decision considering the form he was in at the time. Our best player in Europe that year missing two series did not stack up, although it must be said that Howard and I had had a good run, winning two out of the three matches we played together.

A definite mistake in that match, however, came towards the end of the competition. When we got the half point which meant we retained the trophy, Concorde did a flypast, there were celebrations and everybody forgot about the last three matches still out on the course. Jacklin did not go out either, as far as I remember, and I observed that we still wanted an extra half point actually to *win* the cup. America's Curtis Strange, who as ever had come to win and nothing else, even suggested to Ian Woosnam that they might as well walk in, but Woosie told him that if the Americans won the last three matches, it would be a tie. In the end we did lose all three and the match was tied, which was a shame because we had played well enough to win the competition. It was a mistake on Jacklin's part, although he might argue his job was done because we had retained the cup. I maintain, however, that he should have been booting us up the backside to get out there and pump up the others.

I remember a similar situation very clearly in 1997, when I was assisting Seve at Valderrama. As soon as we were assured of at least a tie, a couple of the caddies jumped in the pond on the seventeenth, and the celebrations started. As soon as they had finished, I said, 'Let's go back and bring in Monty. We want a win not a tie.' Even if Monty had eased up against Scott Hoch, which is unlikely because he always wants to win and that's the right attitude, I wanted to make sure we were out there supporting him.

Jacklin was never one to confide in the team too much. He was usually in the corner whispering to Seve, a very powerful and clever person whose input he obviously considered invaluable. He tended to be dictatorial as a captain, which is not necessarily a bad thing, but I always had the feeling he was telling us what to do and was not prepared to accept our advice about matters. But if Jacklin had his faults, it must also be conceded that he did a brilliant job elevating the Ryder Cup to a different level. He only took the job in the first place on the proviso that the players were upgraded from back of the bus to nose cone. He wanted everything first class. There can be no question: he made a great success of it. When I returned to the Ryder Cup in 1989 after missing the previous three, everything was much better. The players were treated like royalty, and virtually everything to do with the competition – travel, team rooms, hotels, food, etc. – was down to Jacklin. It would probably have happened anyway, but he was the first mover and must get the credit. Before then, most of us had not really thought about it. We just got on a plane assuming we would be turning right. The organisation was, at best, scratchy. Jacklin put his foot down and sorted it out. It was a huge step forward.

By 1989 my relationship with Jacklin was still not brilliant, and part of the reason for this was an incident in the earlier part of the decade. A journalist had approached me and told me Jacklin had said something derogatory about me. I reacted rather rashly, saying he was a pain in the arse, and generally slagged him off. The press had a field day with it, and the story even made *Grandstand*. I only found out later that Jacklin had not said anything of the sort. So I learnt a very important lesson. In future, I would only reply after checking all the facts and making sure I knew exactly what had been said. I went to see Jacklin and apologised. He did not seem too annoyed at the time, but I guess he must have been fairly cross inside, and quite rightly so. What I had done was inexcusable.

But then Jacklin's criticism of Gallacher was equally so. The pair had been friends and colleagues for many years, and had worked together closely during the 1980s when European fortunes took a welcome turn for the better in the Ryder Cup. Bernard was Jacklin's successor, and although he had not been particularly wild about me around the time of the Greenbrier, we had subsequently played many times together and, as far as I was aware, had warmed to each other. While Jacklin always thought like a superstar, Bernard would always talk to the players more and thought more like a tour pro. He got on with his players exceptionally well, and consequently I always felt more comfortable with him. I played under Bernard in three Ryder Cups, and I do not think he did anything wrong. At every stage he took the decision he had to, and I was delighted for him when he won one after twice coming close. Having lost the first two, I do not think he was keen to do it a third time, but he was the players' choice. We were genuinely keen for him to do it again, whereas in 1989 I think Jacklin had pushed himself forward. Without doubt, Jacklin realised that as his career was coming to an end, only as the captain could he maintain his profile and retain a commercial advantage.

Maybe the captain is not as influential and does not quite affect the result as much as some people believe. They can certainly make mistakes, but I do not think Bernard did. We all knew where we were with him, what he was doing and why. He was always realistic without being downbeat, encouraging without being over-enthusiastic – middle of the road emotionally, if you like, which I think is a good thing in a captain. The players understood that and responded, because those three matches produced some very fine golf. The team-room atmosphere under Bernard was always excellent, partly because it was carefully monitored: we were always particular as to who could have access, and normally it was strictly players and wives, although the odd, short visit from a guest was acceptable.

Jacklin and his family came into the team room as Bernard's guests in 1993, and one day one of the most unsavoury incidents I have ever experienced developed. The Belfry staff have always been absolutely brilliant, yet Jacklin never seemed to stop moaning about them, and one morning he came in and just blasted them because the bacon on the breakfast buffet was overcooked. Jane and I could not believe it because he was a guest in there and the staff had been faultless. If he had not liked it he should have gone elsewhere and not kicked up a fuss, but he stayed, and it was really rather unpleasant.

Jacklin certainly had a couple of pops at Bernard's captaincy, which was surprising because they had been pretty good friends. I do not know if they still are, but I guess it is fairly unlikely. To criticise your successor is unforgivable. You can explain how he might have considered other options, but Jacklin could never resist having a go. I know that Bernard, who had entertained Jacklin as a house guest, was not impressed. I think he felt he deserved better treatment, and I can fully understand and sympathise with that sentiment. When you are an ex-captain people will always listen to you, but I think you are better off keeping your mouth shut. It may be a trap I fall into in the coming years, but I am certainly going to try to steer clear.

Jacklin was a studio guest of Sky at the Ryder Cup. The following week at the German Masters, also on Sky, the television station received a number of emails, among which was one that asked if it might not be better to have Seve Ballesteros on air, because he was somebody who actually wanted Europe to win. A lot of players have the feeling that when Jacklin stopped being captain he stopped caring whether Europe won or not. I do not know why that should be the case and I do not understand that attitude, but it is a charge that has been levelled at him by many people.

It was a shame that Jacklin criticised Bernard's captaincy because, as I have said, Bernard never put a foot wrong: there was no dissent in any of the three matches under him and not one player in any of his sides who was not delighted when he finally got his just reward. The 1995 success was not only his first as captain, but mine as a player some eighteen years after my debut. And to win in the USA is simply fantastic. It was something I was not to repeat when my turn came, but it says much of what I thought of Bernard as a captain that many of my words to the boys were similar to things he used to say.

No captain can function properly without able lieutenants, and I knew who I wanted by my side right from the start: my good friend Ken would be ideal in one particular role, and Sam, if he did not qualify as a player, in another. I wanted two people who, if I missed anything or was lacking in any aspect, would pick up on it very quickly, kick me up the backside and say, 'It might be better to do it this way.' With Sam I had a motivator who was extremely popular and highly respected. I knew he would be someone to have a laugh with, up front and noisy with the players and always ready to slap them on the back. He had been there, seen it and done it so many times in the past that his name was inextricably linked with the Ryder Cup. It made perfect sense to have a man with such a big personality there, together with his bubbly wife Suzanne – another great asset for the team room. Sam would help make the players believe they were capable of anything.

With Ken, whose wife Dawn is great fun and mixes brilliantly in all company, I had somebody who was constantly thinking about what he might do to improve our performance and give us an edge, someone who would leave no stone unturned when it came to getting the best out of everybody. Through his role as a Sky commentator and a regular attender on the practice range, he was also familiar with all the players and their games. Ken is the most meticulous man I have ever met. He always treated golf as if it were a game of chess. I needed a grandmaster in the team room, and Ken was ideal for that role because I knew he would not miss one detail. The four of them – Sam, Ken and their wives – were a perfect combination for me, all different characters with unique strengths, united in one aim.

My assistants' qualities turned out to be nothing less than I had expected; they were an enormous help to me and invaluable in every respect. I wanted the position of assistant captain to be a more exalted, more recognisable one because I feel very strongly that assistants are just as important to the team as the captain himself (Ben Crenshaw included Bruce Lietzke and Bill Rogers as his helpers in 1999, because they were hugely respected figures in the USA). I made it clear to our Ryder Cup people that I wanted my assistants to be involved in everything: to be at all the dinners, to walk out at the opening and closing ceremonies, to receive the same gifts as everybody else and generally to be an important part of the team.

We sent off that request to the US PGA, but they wrote back saying that assistant captains would not be allowed to parade with the team at the opening or closing ceremonies and would not be invited to the welcome dinner. Oh, really? We immediately replied, saying that they would physically have to prevent my assistants from walking on at the opening and closing ceremonies if that is what they wanted. I also said that if they were not going to be invited to the welcome dinner, then I would make attendance optional for every member of the team (no prizes for guessing how many players would have gone to it if I had given them a choice). They capitulated. I have no idea why they tried to be stubborn over this matter, but they changed their minds and it was definitely the right decision.

One of my first decisions as captain was to prepare myself for interrogation at the initial press conference announcing my appointment. I knew the throng would want to know why I had agreed to take the job, so I started writing down my reasons. I felt I could do it well, and that it was perhaps a little too soon for the likes of Bernhard Langer, Ian Woosnam and Sam Torrance, all of whom stood a good chance of making the team as players. It was a one-term job, and a foreshortened one at that, with the announcement coming just a year before the match. I also felt that, having played under four captains and been assistant to another, I had the necessary experience, and I was sure Jane would make an excellent lady captain. It had been fully twenty years since the 1979 Ryder Cup, so enough time had elapsed for me to be forgiven for what others may have seen as indiscretions on my part. Murderers do not get terms that long, so a small amount of larking about should have been wiped off the slate in that time. I had decided that was all I would say on that issue, because I wanted nothing to detract from the captaincy itself and the formation of the team.

Finally, I stated that I had every intention of giving the job my full commitment; win, lose or draw, I was determined that my European team would go into the matches better prepared than ever before. To that end I wanted statistics and information, every last little scrap of detail, no matter how insignificant. It was a long list. I asked for every Ryder Cup result; I wanted the points list for each year; the money list at the close of Ryder Cup qualification for each year; weather charts for the Brookline area for September and October for the previous ten years; details and photographs of the course; videos of any major championships held there in the last two decades and performance statistics – driving distance, accuracy, greens in regulation, putts per round – for every player. If there was anything to be learnt from statistical analysis, I wanted to know it.

It must be admitted, though, that I did not glean a huge amount from the mass of statistics. All I discovered, after looking at everything and drawing on my knowledge of players over the years, was that if a side does not have very strong foursomes pairings then without doubt it will lose too many matches for comfort. If there had been any correlation between a golfer's style of play in a particular year and his proficiency at either foursomes or fourballs, I think I would have found it. Foursomes is a very difficult game and, like a lot of other players, I was not particularly good at it, but the bottom line in that particular discipline is that you have to be a very good player. I knew not only that we would need to have the eight best players involved, but that they would need to play well on the day if we were to stand a chance.

My other early decision was to have frequent team meetings during the week. They are always good for airing problems, voicing opinions and raising points. And if we were to have meetings, I realised I had better have something to say when we got there, because it might seem strange if I got up without anything to offer. So I started writing down little titbits of information, and throughout the next few months they turned into a long list which I took with me to Brookline.

But my main concern was that I needed a team. Although I had already been officially elected captain, it would be almost a year before the twelve representatives of the Europe team would be determined.

4 Shaping the Team

ONE OF THE LONGEST-RUNNING STORIES during my term of captaincy revolved around whether I would play if I qualified automatically. It ran and ran and ran – mostly into culs-de-sac. If I had a pound for every word written on the subject, I would now be in a position to buy my own ski slopes, rather than just a new pair of skis.

Truth is, the decision was taken immediately after I accepted the job and never changed once throughout the ensuing twelve months, despite all the many articles. I remember Ken Schofield, the European Tour's chief executive officer, coming up to me after I had been appointed and saying, 'Congratulations, captain. If you get in, you'll play of course.' Those were his exact words, and I replied, 'Absolutely.' There was never a question about whether I would play or not if I qualified, I just did not make it clear from the outset, I suppose because I did not want to do it that way. The press were desperate to know and kept pestering, but I knew the moment I said 'Yes, I'll play if I qualify' they would then want to know who would replace me. Sam was still trying to qualify, so I had asked Ken to be ready to take over. Although he agreed to act as stand-in, he did not want all the fuss and bother that came with the territory. Consequently, no cards had ever been played closer to a chest. I have never had a problem affecting a poker face if necessary, and those who needed to know were the only ones aware of the hand I was holding.

But the way I was playing at the time, I would not have been any use to anyone, particularly because of the way I was putting. To play the Ryder Cup well you need to be confident standing over a three- or four-foot putt. The older I have got, in common with most players, the greater the likelihood of my missing from that range. My performances during 1998 had been miserable, and you can never be certain, particularly in your mid-forties, when your game might enter that spiral of terminal decline.

The thought that I might not have another good year in me had entered my mind before the start of the Ryder Cup year, but I played one event in South Africa at the beginning of February 1999, made the cut and moved on to Dubai, where, for some unknown reason, I started hitting the ball really well. I played consistently and solidly throughout the Desert Classic, and was particularly pleased to finish third. A month later, after a relatively pleasing run, I claimed second place in the Madeira Island Open, and suddenly I had won more than £100,000. The Ryder Cup was certainly not yet in my thoughts from a playing perspective, but I was pleased to be playing well.

Sticking to my schedule saw me heading for the ski slopes rather than the next tee, and when I returned at the end of April for the Spanish Open my brief form had deserted me. I played horrendously in Barcelona, and badly again mid-May during the Benson and Hedges at the Oxfordshire. Even though there was a noticeable improvement in my ball striking at the TPC of Europe in Heidelberg a week later, I still failed to qualify for the weekend action. It was ridiculous. I had had a couple of good weeks of solid play and just could not understand where on earth my form had gone to.

It had nothing to do with being Ryder Cup captain because, apart from being time-consuming, there had been no real bother. Being on the course was actually a relief because it meant nobody could get to me. In fact, I appreciated being out there like never before, because it meant that for up to five hours I could not do any form of interview.

I was in a state of bewilderment by the end of May when I arrived at Wentworth for our most prestigious tour event of the season, the Volvo PGA Championship. It is never the best preparation to arrive at a tournament not knowing whether you are going to hit the fairway or the gallery, but fate had a pleasant surprise waiting for me and I started playing extremely well. The last round would be the best of the lot: I shot a 66 and finished second to Colin Montgomerie. The huge payday of £145,000 rocketed me to seventh in the Ryder Cup list, and suddenly it dawned on me: another £100,000 would give me a chance of making the team – and there were still three months to go.

At the beginning of June, just twelve tournaments away from the team being decided, my form, principally on the back of some appalling putting, deserted me. A good last round in the US PGA Championship in August got me a few ranking points, but I entered the final qualifying event, the BMW International in Munich, needing to finish no lower than second to qualify. It was a task beyond me.

I had run out of tournaments, but never once during the season did I change a schedule which had just one objective: to get me the most money by the end of the year. There was no point in changing emphasis to chase Ryder Cup points because that would almost certainly have been counter-productive. The situation was almost a no-lose one, because although I wanted to make the team I also wanted to captain it, and there is no way anybody can do both. I enjoyed every minute of the build-up throughout the year apart from that last day in Germany, and if, at the end of my career, somebody asks me whether I would have preferred seven Ryder Cup appearances and one captaincy or eight appearances, it would be a very difficult choice to make, but I would probably plump for the former.

Throughout this period when I was attempting to make the team, I was also keeping tabs on all the other contenders. Never at any stage of the process was I in the least bit worried about the way the team was shaping up. The natural process of class finding its way to the top of the list was already well advanced by the start of 1999, several players – all of them predictable – having made the most of the big-money tournaments since qualifying started the previous September. Colin Montgomerie, Lee Westwood and Darren Clarke looked Brookline-bound before striking a ball in the 1999 season, while the Spanish Armada, with José Maria Olazábal and Miguel Angel Jiménez at the helm, was halfway across the Atlantic long before the crucial last few tournaments determined the shape of the team lower down the order.

There were quite a few comments, spoken and written, about how little experience there seemed to be in the team, but none of that worried me. Give me a rookie playing well rather than an older, more experienced player out of form every time. The ten who qualified by right would be Europe's best that year, while my two wild card selections would be the ones I considered best equipped to complement the others, players like Jesper Parnevik, the Swede playing mostly in America and too highly ranked in the world to overlook, and Sergio Garcia, the new Spanish sensation. El Niño was entering the paid ranks on the back of a hurricane rather than a breeze, but had too few opportunities, surely, to make the team automatically. Not for the first time in my life, I was completely wrong.

From the start, and particularly as high summer approached, I was also looking for pointers from players such as Nick Faldo, Bernhard Langer, Ian Woosnam, Costantino Rocca (who had beaten Tiger Woods in the singles at Valderrama), Thomas Bjorn and Per-Ulrik Johansson. Playing well, they would be valuable to the team, but, unfortunately, their form and consistency deserted them too often. I talked to and watched quite a few more as I played with them throughout the year. I think it helped that I was on tour a lot. It may not be essential, but it is helpful if the captain is accessible because players can ask whatever they want in the knowledge that he is in touch with everything that is happening around him.

I was particularly sad that Faldo was going through a rough patch, because I knew that a Faldo playing well would be a huge asset to the team. Nobody amasses a Ryder Cup and individual record like his without having a great deal to offer. The first time I had had much to do with him was in 1977, when we played in the same Ryder Cup team. Paired with Peter Oosterhuis that week, he helped beat Ray Floyd and Lou Graham, and then Floyd and Jack Nicklaus, before rounding it off in style with a superb singles triumph over the reigning Open champion, Tom Watson. It was quite a debut for a twenty-year-old.

Faldo seemed to have everything, even at that early stage. He had good composure, hit the ball straight and a good distance, and possessed a fantastic short game which has remained with him through the years. Although a loner, that was not surprising for somebody entering a whole new world. Ken and I hung around on our own, so we were loners in that respect too, and, like

Faldo, we spent many hours working on our games. Quite often, the only players still on the range towards the end of an afternoon would be me, Ken, Nick and Greg Norman, the great Australian who honed his competitive edge in Europe.

The 1977 Ryder Cup brought Faldo to national prominence, and he went on to realise his potential while always keeping himself to himself. It was a ploy Ken and I tried, but failed at miserably. It would be cruel to say Faldo was not a team player, but he definitely liked to be paired with good players or people he perceived as fellow top performers. After six matches with Oosterhuis he went on to partner double US Masters champion Bernhard Langer as many times, linked up with former world number one and Augusta winner Ian Woosnam for ten matches, record-breaking European number one Colin Montgomerie for seven, and played four with Lee Westwood at a time when the young man from Worksop had already identified himself as a player on the world stage likely to be unfazed by the occasion, even though he was a first-timer at Valderrama.

A lot of us had the feeling Faldo had to be paired with good players; without doubt, his Ryder Cup record would not have been half as impressive had he been paired with me a few times. Only two other players ever partnered Faldo, Sam Torrance and David Gilford, and it was all over very quickly. With Sam he lost 7 & 5 to Lee Trevino and Jerry Pate at Walton Heath in 1981, and with Gilly he went down 7 & 6 at Kiawah Island in 1991 to Paul Azinger and Mark O'Meara. Gilly was playing his first Ryder Cup match that year and needed a bit of help; Faldo was widely criticised for not giving any. He was lucky David's a quiet person and did not take it too personally. To his credit he has said very little about it over the years, but the episode, which few could understand, only added fuel to the feeling that Faldo was more concerned with his own record than the team's. I would like to think he was worried about both and would have done anything to help the team win.

You can say bad things about Nick Faldo, but there is a lot of good there, and I have always found if you asked for advice he gave it. Indeed, I was once the beneficiary of some unsolicited coaching from the player who has three Open claret jugs and as many Augusta green jackets to his credit. During the first morning of the 1993 Ryder Cup there was a fog delay and I was on the practice putting green trying to solve my perennial problems when he wandered over and gave me a few tips. He spent half an hour trying to sort me out, and I was grateful for that because it is always nice to get the advice of somebody who knows what he is talking about.

In 1995, there can be no doubt that what he did in the singles was absolutely fantastic. He turned round his match against Curtis Strange with two great fours on seventeen and eighteen. The one on the last was top-quality: a wedge to five feet and then holing a left-to-right slider showed what he is made of on the course.

Unfortunately, we have not always seen eye to eye off it. One of our more serious clashes was at Woburn in the mid-1990s after Faldo had criticised the European Tour for the standard of its venues. Other players made their feelings about Faldo's observations known to me during a rain delay. They were not just angry, they were absolutely seething, because they felt the attack was unwarranted. They thought it extremely rich that someone who played such a limited European schedule should come out and slag some of our venues. I reacted untypically and, instead of considering it from a dis- tance, went straight to the press room. It was so unlike me: I do not normally go there unless asked. But at that moment I felt the other side of the story needed to be given, and I pointed out that Faldo did not play that many tournaments and that his choice of the ones to play was governed by the amount of prize money on offer and the amount of appearance money that he might receive before a shot had been hit.

The next day Faldo was hitting balls on the range, and when I walked past he spotted me. He came over and confronted me. Anyone could quickly have spotted the fact that he was absolutely furious. Rarely have I seen somebody so cross. The veins were sticking out on his forehead, and he was so red in the face I was sure he was turning into a beetroot. I was equally convinced that, no matter how big the temptation, he would go off his head if I started laughing. I went through what I had told the press and emphasised that he only played in certain tournaments because of the money, citing the Swiss Open as a perfect example. 'You play there, not one of our better courses, so why not others which do have more demanding layouts?' I asked. 'It isn't because of the money, but a watch contract,' he replied. I said, 'That's exactly what I mean. It's money-orientated, case proved.'

That was the end of it. It just seemed incredible to me, because although it is one thing to make an honest criticism about the tour, I always believe it should be done behind closed doors. Secondly, what he was saying was from a very flimsy base, given that his schedule was driven by remuneration or incentives. I would never say there is nothing wrong with the tour, but things improve every year. If Faldo had a real beef about something he should have taken it to Ken Schofield or the committee, because if a player of his standing in the game comes along and starts saying things, people generally listen and will sit down and debate the issues.

I once read somewhere that Faldo's idea of dining out was dinner for one on the balcony of his hotel bedroom, and that does seem believable. People do have very limited contact with him because you rarely see him, even if you are staying at the same hotel. Nobody ever gets the chance to discover what he is really like.

Nevertheless, I was determined at the start of the 1999 season to keep an open mind about Faldo. He had been in a bit of a slump, but was making every attempt to come out of it. I even said in the press: 'Nick is doing all the right things, working very hard and saying what a captain wants to hear.' I tried to go out of my way to be positive about Faldo because I knew he would be a huge asset to the side if he returned to form.

Our paths had not crossed for some time until we were paired together for the first two rounds of the Benson and Hedges at the Oxfordshire. I enjoy his company on the course because it is always helpful to watch an expert in action. Even if he is playing badly, there is always something you can learn from a master of his craft, and that is an apt description of Faldo. I was continually being asked by the press about him, so I thought it best to make my position perfectly clear to him before we played in case anything I said was misrepresented. I told him I wanted him in the team, but that he would have to show some form. I made it quite plain that if he read anything else, or, indeed, anything negative, then there was every chance I had not said it at all. Some players complain that Faldo does not speak to them on the course, but I view that as his prerogative. When I have played with him he has tended not to initiate conversations, but if you talk to him, as I did that day, he will respond. But that was the last time I spoke to him before the last counting event, the BMW in Germany.

The one thing I was always very careful to avoid was any conflict with the players in the run-up to or during the Ryder Cup. I felt it important to create a good atmosphere at all times, and I wanted everybody to know exactly where they stood. I followed the progress of all the players who had a chance of making the team, even those with a claim for a wild card position. I wanted to know as much as possible about all of them before we arrived in Brookline.

Faldo soon virtually disappeared from my thinking because he had not shown any form worth thinking about, and many others had better claims to the Ryder Cup places. Faldo is such a talented player that if he shows any signs at all of form he will finish in the top three, but there were precious few top twenties, never mind top tens. As we approached the last counting event, I was not even thinking of him as a possible wild card. Even if he won the last event he would still be outside the top fifteen in the points list, and I had made it clear from the start that I would neither pick nor discount anybody on the form of one tournament.

Before the weekend of BMW week, Faldo was quoted in the press as saying he could not believe I had not spoken to him about his chances of a wild card, but it had never occurred to me. Nobody in the past had ever broached such a matter with me. You do your best and make your choices in my view, but he slagged me off for it. He did not have it out with me personally, but went straight to the press and gave me a damn good slating. I thought it most peculiar, as did everybody else, including the Fourth Estate. The players in the bar found it ironic, to say the least, that he should complain about my not talking to him. Several said, 'It's amazing, because he hasn't talked to anybody for the last ten years on tour.'

That evening we bumped into each other in the hotel foyer, and he asked me for a quick word. I told

him that even if he won that week it was 'unlikely' –
and that was the exact word I used – that I would give
him a wild card. He muttered 'All right' and wandered
off. Faldo approached me again the following morning
as he walked towards the practice green. He said: 'Can
you repeat what you said last night so that I can get it
clear in my own mind?' I told him exactly the same as I
had the previous evening. 'Oh!' he said, and walked off.

After the round he slagged me off again to the press
for telling him that. I was perplexed; I just could not
work out exactly what he wanted to hear. If I had said,
'If you win or come second you have a real chance of
a wild card,' and he had done that and I had still not
selected him, then he would have gone absolutely ape.
I felt I was being honest when I used the word
'unlikely', because I could not be sure whether or not I
would have handed him a wild card had he won. A
victory would have made some sort of case, but not
necessarily a conclusive one. He would still have been
too far down the list. The only player I would have
been prepared to go past a few names to select would
have been Sergio Garcia, but he had taken that option
out of my hands by forcing himself into the side in
unbelievable style.

A lot of players, including me, do not understand
Faldo. He can say such strange things, although I do
feel he has been given a raw deal by the press. He has
been criticised a lot, and I believe that is one of the
main reasons why he has gone to play in the USA,
where he does not get jumped on for every little thing
he does or does not do. But it is not always easy to
sympathise with him. I remember cringing when he
won the Open at Muirfield for the second time. He had
won it brilliantly, and he was everybody's hero. Then
he made a speech in which he thanked several people
from the bottom of his heart and the press from the

heart of his bottom before breaking out into song. It was incredible. One minute you were admiring the guy completely, and half an hour later you were left wondering what planet he was from.

Faldo has said in the past that one day he would like to be the Ryder Cup captain, but I think that will depend a lot on his relationship with the players. A lot of them do not like him because he has been critical of the European Tour, keeps himself so much to himself, and tends not to acknowledge people. If he seeks his own company and wants to keep his head down without saying hello to anybody then that is his business and I have absolutely no problem with it, but I do think a player like that fits in better on the US Tour. On the European circuit we expect people to stop and have a chat a bit more. It is just the way things are.

The good thing is that these days the captain is chosen at a joint meeting of the committee and the board, and the committee is extremely representative of the players – more so now than ever before. Somebody the players do not particularly get on with will probably not make a good captain, and I think unless Faldo's relationships with others improve, I doubt he would ever be elected. Just because he has achieved what he has does not automatically qualify him for the captaincy. And let there be no misunderstanding: Faldo is hugely talented and has kept himself in good shape. He has the desire and will to search endlessly for the right stuff to make a comeback. I hope he does, because if he qualifies for the next team, I am sure it will be to the benefit of the European team. I am sure that Faldo thinks I do not ever want to see him play in the Ryder Cup again, but that, as I have said, is simply not true. I have a lot of admiration for him as a player and would love to see him up there again challenging for the game's big prizes.

The bottom line is that if Faldo is playing well, you want him in your side. In the build-up to Brookline he was not, and I did not pick him for that reason.

The only other player who talked to me about wild card selection was Sweden's Per-Ulrik Johansson, who had played in two winning teams but had not had a great season by his own standards. At the US PGA he wanted to know whether or not I would select him if he came over to Germany and won and finished eleventh on the points list. I could not give him a guarantee, but I did say it would be difficult to ignore him. He went to Germany and tried, but for Per-Ulrik it was not to be.

What had originally looked like being an easy decision in terms of the wild card places, with Parnevik and Garcia getting the nod, was turned into one of great difficulty when the young Spaniard shocked everybody by finishing second to Tiger Woods in the final major championship of the season. As soon as he won in July in Ireland after just a handful of starts in the professional ranks I knew he was going to be difficult to overlook as a wild card, but by running Woods close in the US PGA and moving straight into the top ten he took himself right out of that equation.

A ton of paracetamol would not have been enough to deal with the headaches that came with having to make a new second choice. I discussed the situation with Colin Montgomerie, Ken and Sam, but ultimately it was my decision, my responsibility. There were only three serious candidates: Bernhard Langer, a veteran of many matches and a fierce matchplay competitor, and two rookies, Scotland's Andrew Coltart and Sweden's Robert Karlsson. Although Bernhard had had better results than Faldo, he had not had many good ones between the PGA at Wentworth and the BMW and was not hitting the ball well. I simply could not justify his selection to myself, as much as I would have loved to have him in the side. Had he finished eleventh in the list it would have been simple, but he did not, and it was not. Andrew and Robert had both played well throughout the year, and it was as tough as it gets deciding between them. It was almost a question of tossing a coin.

Had I selected Robert, who had pipped Andrew to eleventh place in the final counting event, nobody could have complained, and few would have raised much objection had I decided to take Bernhard, because most people's fears about the team (not mine) were to do with its lack of experience. There was a precedent for going further down the qualification list to find a wild card – when I was selected in 1991 I had finished eighteenth in the table – but on this occasion I had already decided that Garcia was probably the only one I would go lower than twelfth to sign up.

Eventually I had to make a choice, and I decided that over a period of two months or so building up to the cut-off point, Andrew had shown more consistency. His golf had been solid all year, and he played well under pressure, never changing his routine and remaining level-headed throughout. He would be able to take his normal game to Brookline, and that is all you want in a Ryder Cup. Later, people asked why I did not play him until the final day. The answer was there in the list. We had the season's top ten players there, so to put in Andrew on the first day ahead of somebody who finished seventh or eighth would not have been right. The way things transpired he did not get a look-in until the last day, but that is the way the chocolate-chip cookie crumbles. If the three who sat it out until the Sunday thought they were badly done by, then imagine how John Garner must have felt after qualifying for the Ryder Cup teams of 1971 and 1973. He played just one series in the first match and not at all in the second at a time when not every player necessarily played in the singles.

If coming to the final decision was extremely difficult, it was easy compared to having to tell both Bernhard and Robert after the BMW International that all their efforts to make the team had been in vain. Nevertheless, the task had to be faced and I knew it came with the territory when I accepted the job. Much as I had already enjoyed my term of captaincy, after I spoke to my two colleagues I realised it was a job I would not want to do again. Without question, talking to the two of them was the hardest thing I have had to do in my professional life.

I have a tremendous respect for Bernhard, not only because of what he has achieved in the game, but because of the way he has gone about becoming a truly great champion. There was no easy way of breaking the news, neither was there a particularly appropriate place to do it. In the end I had to settle for a small space between two marquees. It was the only private place I could find on the spur of the moment, but unfortunately it turned out to be exactly the opposite. Just as I was explaining to Bernhard that I had decided not to select him a Sky Sports cameraman spotted us and immediately trained his lens in our direction, believing he was eavesdropping on an exclusive. They could not pick up the dialogue, but anchorman David Livingstone immediately came to the conclusion that I was handing out good news. I considered it intrusive in the first place for a private chat to be filmed like that, but then to get things as wrong as they could possibly be *on air* was unforgivable. While Sky viewers were hearing how I was bringing good news to Bernhard, Bernhard knew it was anything but.

I knew exactly how Bernhard felt because I had suffered similarly in the past when in the running for a

Ryder Cup place. He took the news exactly as I thought he would, like the man and gentleman that he is, but the disappointment ran deep in his eyes. If he said anything I cannot remember it, but I was in a high state of emotion myself and struggling to say the right things.

A short time afterwards I found Robert Karlsson and took him to the same place. As with Bernhard, I considered the highly talented Swede a friend and knew it would be just as difficult to break the bad tidings to him. In fact it was even more so: Robert was absolutely gutted, a feeling I was becoming all too familiar with. If Bernhard was surprised, Robert was in shock. He just could not believe what he was hearing. I think he could have accepted it had I gone down the list to Bernhard, but he could not take in why he had to lose out to anybody else.

He still had not come to terms with it when we met again a couple of hours later at the airport. It was an impromptu meeting; we were on different flights, but we left from adjoining gates. As soon as Robert saw me he came over and asked me to run through everything again. It was just as difficult the second time around, possibly harder, because I could tell he did not accept my reasoning. By the time we parted to board our separate flights, I was completely drained. I have never felt worse in my life. It may have been only a short flight back to Manchester, but it felt like an eternity. I said very little, but I was extremely pleased to have Jane by my side. It had been an extremely unpleasant task for all concerned, and I just wanted to get home and have a week off.

The only person I had not had a chance to talk to was the only one I had good news for. I had somehow missed Andrew, but I rang him later that evening, and for the first and only time that day a smile returned to my face. Andrew had first heard the news from one of our European Tour colleagues just as he was about to board his flight to Heathrow. English World and Alfred Dunhill Cup player Richard Boxall has something of a reputation as a practical joker, and when he told Andrew that his father had just been on the phone to say that he had heard of Andrew's selection on television, there was a suspicion of it being a wind-up. Boxy assured him it was not, and although by the time I phoned Andrew was pretty much convinced he was in the team, I think he was still pleased to hear it from me.

When Bernard Gallacher selected me in 1991 after going quite a few spots down the list, I had said to him, 'I won't let you down.' He had replied, 'I know you won't.' This phone call with Andrew was a definite case of *déjà vu*: when I told him he was a wild card he simply said, 'I won't let you down,' to which I replied, 'I know you won't.' It was not the first or last time I would use one of Bernard's lines with the team.

Rarely have I been more pleased to fall into my own bed, but I woke up the next morning with a strange tingling down the fingers of my left hand and through my arm, which had what looked like a little bite by the elbow. I thought nothing of it, and assumed I had probably slept on it. A day later I was still not feeling great, but I put it down to tiredness and needing some rest after all the trauma and stress. Still it persisted, and by the Wednesday there was a dull ache in the elbow and other spots were developing. I did not think it worth bothering the doctor with, so I went to the chemist and was given some anti-histamines. The pain persisted, though. By the weekend my elbow was really hurting and a rash was developing near my wrist. I still stayed away from the doctor's, and come Sunday morning the pain was not only killing me, but heading towards my shoulder.

Although I knew practically nothing about shingles, I started to think that that was what it might be, for no other reason than the rash and the tingling sensation. My first thought as I hot-footed it towards Otley Hospital was that my arm was infected so badly they might have to amputate. I knew I could eke out a living on the regular tour on the way to the seniors, but you do not make much money on the one-armed tour. Shingles was in fact the diagnosis, but I had had it too long for treatment to be effective so there was nothing to do other than take pain-killers – and they did not help much. At least, my friends reassured me, I would be over it in a week.

High temperatures and further pain forced me to miss several functions the following week, but gradually I began to feel a lot better. As soon as it became clear I was not going to need an artificial limb, the same friends who had been so supportive called back to say, 'Did you know that had the rash joined up around your body, your head would have dropped off?' and, 'Some people even go blind.' I have such wonderful friends.

I came out of the illness convinced, by Jane, that everything had been caused by the stress of the week in Germany – not just by my interviews with Bernhard Langer and Robert Karlsson, but by going into the tournament myself having to finish in the top two to make the side, and coming a desperately close fifth instead. At least I now felt fit and healthy again, ready to take what I was sure was Europe's best possible team – Darren Clarke, Andrew Coltart, Sergio Garcia, Padraig Harrington, Miguel Angel Jiménez, Paul Lawrie, Colin Montgomerie, José Maria Olazábal, Jesper Parnevik, Jarmo Sandelin, Jean Van de Velde and Lee Westwood – to Brookline in the USA.

5 Us and the US

THERE IS SOMETHING ABOUT Colin Montgomerie which sets him apart. He is regarded as the leader of the players, a big man with a big game and personality to match. There is no subject on which Monty does not have an opinion, but he is far from blinkered and always sees both sides. He will hold up his hands if he is wrong just as much as he will press his point if he believes he is right.

Monty has played so well for so long – seven successive European Tour Order of Merit titles speak for themselves – that the other players respect him enormously, not just because he is such a good golfer, but because he has been so loyal to the tour. They know there is someone in the team who is always going to perform whatever the occasion and demands. We just knew he was going to play well at Brookline, that he would do it with and against anybody. Had I said, 'I want you to play with so-and-so because I think it is in the team's best interest,' he would have accepted it without question, regardless of his partner's world ranking or status within the game.

In Europe, Monty is without doubt our Tiger Woods. He hits the ball a long way, further than most might appreciate, and his iron play is so good because not only does he hit it in the direction he wants, but he gets the desired distance too, and that is not only a craft in itself, but one he has mastered in the late 1990s. Earlier on he was still winning the money list, but not always hitting his shots the distance he wanted. Now he is in control. There are few better chippers than Monty, and he is a very, very good putter, definitely better than he gives himself credit for. There are times when he appears not to hole much, but when a player is hitting as high a percentage of greens in regulation as Monty does, it is very difficult to look as if you are holing regularly.

Nobody present, or watching on television, will ever forget his comeback against Mark Calcavecchia at the 1991 Ryder Cup. In those days his stock shot was a low cut, he had problems drawing the ball and was not particularly long either – far from the player he is today – but from dormie four down he hung on, the American collapsed, and Monty turned what was an odds-on defeat into a half. Since then, he has turned that low cut into a perfectly flighted fade and can now hit the ball either way off the tee or with his irons. He appears to have every shot in the book and, without changing his swing, has conquered all his earlier problems.

Monty arrived on tour in the late 1980s with a swing which was certainly not textbook and at a time when the theories of coach David Leadbetter were just taking off. It is to his credit that he was not one of the huge number of people misinterpreting the Leadbetter method. Golfers were putting towels under their arms and hitting drivers on the range; others were putting beach balls between their legs for some strange reason. I asked David about the towels-under-arms drill, and he said he was equally amazed at what people were doing because that particular training technique was meant to accompany three-quarter nine-iron shots only. It would prove a disaster for all those who believed it helped every shot: misinterpreting things can be worse than not doing anything at all. Monty managed to avoid that particular pitfall. He never really went off his own track, refining things here and there when necessary, but basically sticking to what he had. If he was coming on tour now, you might look at his swing and think there were one or two things to look at, but it just shows that you can still get to the top by sticking with something you know.

There is a lesson in what Monty has done for everybody who turns professional: see how far you can go with what you have, and if you decide you are not going far enough, then and only then try to change things. All Monty has done is improve a few of the basics, but his is still not what anybody would call a textbook swing. All the same, it is very powerful, affords great accuracy and manifests exceptional rhythm. It just shows what you can do with a little tweak here and there, and I believe in the last few years coaches generally have been a lot more willing to allow a player to keep his natural swing and then just try to make sure the fundamentals can fit in, rather than starting from scratch and rebuilding.

We knew that at Brookline the rest of the team would look to Monty for a lead, and he would give it. No matter whom he partnered it would be a good pairing, and once you have a player like that it gives the rest confidence. But if Monty was the leader by example, nobody commanded more respect in the team room than José Maria Olazábal. Winner of two Augusta green jackets and a host of other tournaments, the Spaniard was our most experienced Ryder Cup campaigner. Olly's presence was felt just as much in the confines of the hotel and locker room as on the course, his fabulous sense of humour topped only by the warmth he exudes as he jokes and enjoys life with the rest of the boys. He has been where it matters an awful lot, performed under pressure and always got a little bit more out of himself in high-pressure situations. Although he must have learnt a lot from Seve Ballesteros, he is an inspirational character in his own right who has evolved his own way and become not only his own man, but also very valuable to the cause. It is a great feeling for a captain to have somebody like him in the side.

When he had his illness in the mid-1990s, it was as if the entire tour was in mourning. He was only 29, coming into his prime, and everybody was just hoping he would get his health back. We were all delighted when he did recover, and when he won his second green jacket at Augusta, his place in the team was guaranteed. Olly went to Brookline not playing particularly well, so I was delighted to see John Jacobs, father of the European Tour and a distinguished player and coach, on the plane. If anybody could get Olly back to form, it was John. He had four days to bring about some sort of improvement.

There were no such worries with Paul Lawrie, the Scot who had stunned the golfing world at Carnoustie in July by winning the Open Championship, having started the final day ten shots behind. I spoke to Monty about Paul a couple of times before the Ryder Cup and we both had the feeling that, although he was obviously a very good player, he might be special under pressure. Monty was happy to play with him, and I had no problem with that because, with all the old pairings no longer in the team, we had to find some new ones. We saw Paul as being unflappable and a very good chipper and putter, qualities of immense value in pressure situations. In fact, some of the players call him Chippy because of his outstanding short game, and we knew how important that area of the game would be.

Paul, relatively unknown outside Europe before his Open triumph, had not received as much credit as I thought he deserved after his success on the east coast of Scotland. People said he came from nowhere on the last day, got a good round in and then watched others throw the silver claret jug at him. That argument would hold water but for two things. While everybody else appeared to be overwhelmed by the last four holes, Paul, not just once but twice, played them magnificently. To make three at seventeen and eighteen the way he did was nothing short of tremendous considering the severe pressure he must have been under. The way he won the Open and the way he coped with the adulation afterwards was nothing short of first class too. (Former US PGA champion Davis Love said the Open got the champion it deserved, but Davis does come out with some daft things now and again, I believe, and that was a particularly unpleasant one to boot. He also said after the Ryder Cup that we, including me, were bad losers. That is something I have never been accused of before because, actually, I am an expert at losing. I have had a lifetime's training at it.)

Paul would go on to confirm his emergence as a player of the highest order by leading the World Series in Akron, Ohio, for two rounds on his first visit to the USA, which was a heck of a performance. Sam Torrance and I both played with him at the K-Club in his first tournament after the Open, and we were both impressed. He did not play particularly well, but the way he fashioned a score when he was not at his best was notable. He shot under par both days, his bad shots were not destructive, and when he missed the green he would get up and down.

I played with him again mid-September at the Lancôme in Saint-Nom-La-Breteche, and although he did not play particularly well again, he stayed in contention. All the top players in Europe over the last twenty years have managed to do that. If they have a bad day they shoot 71, whereas if I have one it is a 74. That has always been the difference between me and the top players. It has nothing to do with ball striking, merely the ability to turn a poor round into a 71 and still be able to clock up a high finish.

I had no worries about throwing Paul and Monty into the high-pressure zone, but some doubts were cast over Jean Van de Velde after what happened to him at the Open: a double-bogey six up the last hole would have been enough to take the win, but he took seven. Personally I had faith in the Frenchman because he did absolutely everything right at Carnoustie for 71 holes and two shots. I could see exactly what he was trying to do coming up the eighteenth, and I think he did the right thing in taking a driver and going for it. Had his approach not hit a grandstand and then ricocheted back short of the Barry Burn, he would probably have won, so I think it was merely a question of fate taking over. Pressure at the Open or anywhere else does not start on the last hole; it begins when you are leading after three rounds, as Jean was. That is when it starts to get to you, and the manner in which he dealt with it was fantastic.

I know he was disappointed at not playing until the singles at the Ryder Cup, because I am certain he felt he had more to prove than anybody else in the team. He wanted to show the Open was no flash in the pan and that he is a very good player. I have known Jean for a long time and I am sure he will go on to do exactly that. I know his game and how he plays: he is long enough, fairly straight, solid with his irons, his short game is very good, and when his putter gets going he can hole from anywhere. He has no weaknesses, and that is his strength, as it is quite often with all very good players.

I am sure Jean thinks that I do not have a high regard for his game, but that is not the case. He said a couple of things after the Ryder Cup which could have been deemed critical of my captaincy, but there are no hard feelings and we get on fine. I could understand his disappointment: he wanted to prove to the Americans that he was not just a crazy Frenchman who ended up taking his shoes and socks off and going for a paddle in the Barry Burn at the Open. Whatever Jean said and thought afterwards he was never less than supportive of the team throughout, and he was a great character for the players' room.

Nobody expected Miguel Angel Jiménez to be another character, but that is what he turned out to be. At 35 he has been round the block several hundred times in his Ferrari, and I had seen him develop as a player in the mid to late 1990s. He had turned from somebody who wafted it with a weakish cut to a player who had eradicated all his weaknesses and become highly skilled in all departments, while retaining a cool head. I had a feeling Mechanico, as we call him, would prove an invaluable player, and he was. (I think he believes he has that nickname because of his rather mechanical action. In fact, he was dubbed Mechanico because he has the appearance of somebody who would look more at home with his head under a car bonnet checking the plugs and sump oil while messing about with the carburettor. I am not sure if anybody had told him that prior to the Ryder Cup. They have now, but it is a soubriquet we use very affectionately because he has everybody's respect as a player and a person.)

I was very confident he would be able to perform because although he was a rookie, he had played a lot and was Seve's deputy in Valderrama. Without question, I thought he was good enough to play all five series. He was, and he did. Having three Spaniards in the side did not make me worried in the slightest that it created an imbalance. If they all played like Miguel,

I would have been happy with twelve Spaniards. I knew him, if not that well, before the Ryder Cup, but you all get to know one another an awful lot more during the week of the match, and that was definitely the case with Miguel. What we saw and heard was a delight. He had the others cracking up in interview situations because he has mastered the technique of failing to understand English if there is something he does not want to answer. But Miguel answered all his questions on the course, and that was all that mattered.

The third Spaniard was no less a figure than Sergio Garcia, who would have been, as I have mentioned, one of the wild cards had he not quite made it under his own steam. I had not played with him before the Ryder Cup, but had seen him on the range and spoken to a lot of people about him. He had been in my thoughts from the beginning of my captaincy, even though at that time he was still an amateur. I wanted to know what people thought of him. I purposely did not speak to Seve, because when you are close to somebody it can be difficult to offer an objective opinion, but those I did speak to were of the same opinion, and every comment was positive. In fact, I quizzed virtually everyone who had ever been paired with him on his style of play, temperament and anything else I could think of at the time. I had all the information I could possibly gather, and even if he did occasionally spray the ball he was already an outstanding iron player and an excellent putter.

Sergio's enormous talent had already been seen on the world stage, and I knew that whatever happened in qualification he needed to be put in the side. Although still a teenager, his strength of game and personality made him a candidate for playing all five series. Apart from a great long game, he has that touch and nerve on the greens players tend only to have when they are relatively young. He has not missed that many four-footers as a result of dribbling them up to the hole.

Sergio wanted to play with Jesper Parnevik, and I was more than happy to grant that wish. I have played with the slightly eccentric Swede over the years and seen him develop to the stage where he now commands the respect of everybody who plays with him. His game has no holes, and few hit the ball straighter. I thought he would be the perfect foil. It was always going to be difficult for Jesper to qualify as of right because of the limited number of appearances he made in European team counting events, but all the other players looked up to him and thought he should be included, and I agreed. Jesper is not one to jump up and down and swing from chandeliers, but after he played his first Ryder Cup in 1997 he realised what all the fuss was about and wanted to be part of it very badly. I was just as willing to accommodate him and told him during the US PGA Championship that he did not have to play the BMW the following week to try to qualify because I had already decided he would get a wild card.

It looked like Padraig Harrington might not figure on the potential invitation list, but two second-place finishes got him in at the last minute, and what a valuable member of the team he proved. It would have been difficult to ignore him anyway because what he did to make the team under pressure was extremely characterful. I was also convinced he would take that form with him to Brookline, because when he plays well it tends to be over a number of weeks rather than just in short, sharp bursts. The Irishman's strengths have generally been his chipping and putting, but before and during the competition he was doing everything well, including hitting the ball a long way and straight. He was also one of our players – Miguel Angel Jiménez was another – whose qualities the Americans were underestimating. It just shows how wrong you can be. Both showed they are right up there, and will be for a long time.

If I knew what to expect of Padraig, I was not as certain about Jarmo Sandelin because over the years he has taken the normal parameters of eccentricity and pushed them to new limits. It has been difficult for most of us on the tour to know what to make of him, and I wondered what he would be like in a team environment. I had never really socialised with him and consequently did not know him, so I made it my job in the run-up to try to discover what made him tick. To achieve that I had to do something I had never previously tried: I fiddled the draw at the Lancôme because I wanted to play with him and Paul Lawrie.

On the Thursday morning before the first round he spotted me on the practice green, came over and said, 'Next week, Jesse [my nickname], anything you need from me, I will give it.' The way he said it, a certain tone in his voice, made me realise I would have no problems with him at Brookline. Indeed, once there, we got to know Jarmo's little idiosyncrasies and greatly appreciated them.

Jarmo had obviously been thinking about the Ryder Cup. During practice with friends, he encouraged them to shout at the top of his backswing and generally make a noise so that he would be able to cope if confronted with the problem in Brookline. He was obviously a canny operator.

One of Jarmo's strengths is the number of birdies he makes, and I would not have had any problem throwing him into the fourballs if anybody had wanted a break or was off form. As it happened, Jarmo, Andrew and Jean did not play until the final day, which was a pity, but that is life.

One player I was convinced would play all five series was Lee Westwood. He is such a good player and so controlled mentally that it is extremely easy to have him in the team. He reminds me very much of Sandy Lyle in his early days. The simplicity of their thought processes was very similar, but that is not to say they are not clever, just that they play golf with a lot of common sense. Some professionals cannot see the wood for the trees into which they have just hit their ball, but Lee sees things quickly and easily. With a bagful of tournament wins around the world, I knew he could perform under pressure, but he is also good fun in the team room.

Lee has the full package – breakfast, lunch and dinner – but probably his biggest strength is that he hits so few destructive shots. In this respect he is possibly the only player who can top Monty, and he does it better than anybody I have seen for a long time. He is that good. When I played with him in Holland during the 1999 season he was no better than poor on the first day and not much better the second, but still he did not hit one destructive shot, firing a 72 and a 68. To do that on a course like Hilversum where you have to walk down a few fairways single file is very impressive. He went on to win there, as he has everywhere he has played, so now he just has the majors to go at. I believe he could claim any of them, such is his all-round strength, but the problem is that majors are definitely overrated and occasionally have their courses tricked up. That does not suit the best players, just the best putters. The US Open is a perfect example of that because many times over the past twelve years it has been reduced, in many players' opinions, to near farce.

There was little doubt who Lee wanted to be paired with. Both he and his close friend Darren Clarke had expressed a wish to team up, and they had even been practising for the possibility. During the third round of the NEC World Championship event in Akron at the end of August they had swapped caddies, such was their determination to have all angles covered come the big week.

The word 'mercurial' describes Darren perfectly. He can be extremely positive and just as negative. His mental attitude is often dictated by the way he is playing, and if he does have a problem it is here. I knew it would be a big help to him if we had a good team atmosphere with everybody happy and enjoying the week. If that happened, then I was sure Darren would be ready to play. When he is tuned in, it is difficult to think of anything he does not do well because he has a huge talent, hits the ball long and straight, can go high or low with his irons and has a very good putting stroke. If he and Lee wanted to play together, so be it.

With the eleventh-hour selection of Andrew Coltart, whose merits I extolled in the previous chapter, I had my team, but I had given precious little thought to the opposition before we got there. Whatever their twelve, I knew captain Ben Crenshaw would be confident he had enough firepower to win back Sam Ryder's precious pot of gold.

There were few, if any, weaknesses in their line-up. I thought if any of their side would not play until the singles it would be Mark O'Meara, because he would be the first to admit he had not had such a good year, after winning two majors the previous season. I also knew, with his experience, that if he did hit form he could putt the eyes out of the course. And if I had reservations about anybody else in the US team, it was Justin Leonard; I wondered if the course would suit his game, especially as he had not played particularly well in the run-up to the competition. I thought being shorter off the tee than many of the others and not hitting the ball as high might work against him, but having said that he was no four-handicapper and his barren spell had not been that long. The fact that I isolated two very good players in this respect was a tribute to how strong the Americans were.

Payne Stewart had won the US Open that summer, and his nerve could not be doubted, but he had not played particularly well since, which was not too surprising. I did feel, too, that he was potentially one of the weaker members of their side. I had studied their statistics and Payne was running 140th in greens in regulation and second in putting, which told the story of his year: up and down with his long game, deadly on the shaved grass. But although he was not playing well I knew he would be an asset to the team because of his character. There was never any bullshit with him. Whatever he said you believed because he could always back it up with facts and arguments. He was a good, hard man to have on your side, particularly useful in the team room.

Elsewhere it was difficult to find anybody who was not on form, or who might not be suited by the insistence of the course on long and straight hitting. Hal Sutton had played well for a long time and was bang in form in the run-up, so he was obviously going to be a solid team member. Jeff Maggert, who made the team as the world matchplay champion having won the million-dollar jackpot at the Andersen Consulting event in Carlsbad, California, earlier in the year, was also a strong player. And I thought Steve Pate a very wise pick as a wild card. Indeed, in Ben's shoes I would have chosen exactly the same two wild cards, because nobody could have argued against Tom Lehman either (the arguments with him would come later). Steve had played well all year; with his nerve and ability to play under pressure he was a must for the team. Tom had struggled with his game, but was starting to come good at the right time. I thought he would play a good few games because he is a strong man and a proven performer under pressure at the highest level – exactly what you want in a Ryder Cup situation.

I had not paid a huge amount of attention to how the American players had been performing, but I knew I had not seen much of Jim Furyk's name, although that was probably because I had been looking at the wrong list. He is usually up there in the top ten every week; if he is not, you assume he took a week off.

There was no lack of knowledge when it came to Tiger Woods, though. He was continuing to prove that the game had a new phenomenon. He had been creeping away from the rest of the golfing world, and in the world rankings had moved into a league of his own. He has the temperament and game to do what Nicklaus did in the 1960s and 1970s. He may not equal Jack's record of eighteen majors, but he will be a dominating force in them. It is harder to win the big ones these days because players work harder and are fitter, and the net has been cast wider, but if anybody can then it is Tiger. Although still not 24 before the Ryder Cup started, Tiger had already collected two major championships and the respect of golfers the world over. He had also matured immeasurably since the time he first appeared on the professional scene, when I had the feeling he was being influenced too much by men in suits and minority pressure groups. The problems he had with a comment made by Fuzzy Zoeller were a typical example.

After Tiger won the Masters in 1997, Fuzzy, a former Masters and US Open champion, quipped that Tiger would probably be serving fried chicken and collard greens at his champion's dinner the following year. I could not believe the furore that followed, and a lucrative contract with KMart disappeared with it. I have known Fuzzy for many years; he might be good at taking the mickey, but racist he is not. I think the uproar which followed that comment was ridiculous. Had it been Sandy Lyle, and had Fuzzy said 'He'll be serving haggis, or whatever the Scots eat', nobody would have had a problem.

I was at Valderrama for the 1999 World Golf Championship event, and Notah Begay, a rare native American Indian on the US Tour, was on the putting green when Tiger walked past. It was a beautiful day, and Tiger said, 'Hi, Notah. Working on your tan?' It was not racist, just a joke, and in the same bracket as Fuzzy's comment. The South African player John Bland was always winding up Fiji's Vijay Singh when the pair of them played in Europe. Blandy was always telling Vijay to eat white chocolate so that he did not bite any of his fingers off. It was not racism, just an amusing comment about the way a person looks, whether it is skin colour or a big nose. I have never come across any form of racism on the European Tour. We play with so many different races it just has never been a factor. And I know what racism is because I have experienced it in South Africa, a country I have been to at least twenty times since I turned professional in 1976. Indeed, I was banned by Sweden for a number of years in the mid-1980s because they would not permit entry to people who had played in South Africa (subsequently, I have never felt any duty to play the Swedish tournaments). I have been aware of racism and seen it in action, but on tour all the players treat one another with respect, and that is how it should be.

It took Tiger a year or two to find his feet and start to make the right decisions for himself, and now he does a tremendous job. I believe he will become an outstanding ambassador for the game as Jack Nicklaus and Arnold Palmer have been.

Of the others in Ben's team, Phil Mickelson and Davis Love, to me, were in a similar category – dangerous campaigners suited to a course playing long – as was David Duval, the world number two, who had gone off the boil a bit compared to his early-season form. All three would be key players.

All in all, I felt they had a very good, well-balanced, experienced team, but I was not going to say so in the build-up. I also thought we had nothing to feel inferior about. Jesper called us the under-puppies, but he and I knew there was a bite running all the way through our team. The standard of our golf would bear testimony to that.

6 Brookline Bond

T HE TIME BETWEEN THE ANNOUNCEMENT of the teams and the start of the week of the 33rd Ryder Cup went by quickly, but there was plenty to occupy my time and thoughts before we got there. I was anxious to ensure I had missed nothing which might contribute towards a successful week. It was also important that everybody knew what they were doing, what was expected of them and what they were likely to encounter in what was going to be an emotionally charged atmosphere. The last thing I wanted was to arrive in Boston and be faced with new problems.

I had long intended to sit down and have an in-depth talk with my immediate predecessors, Seve Ballesteros and Bernard Gallacher, but for whatever reason – principally lack of time and opportunity – it had not been possible. I finally caught up with Bernard in Brookline, but I was indebted to a spot of quick thinking by my assistant, Ken Brown, for the chance to share a glass of Rioja with Seve – and what an enlightening and entertaining evening it turned out to be.

Ken spoke to me the week before the Lancôme Trophy and suggested that it might be a good idea to have a pre-Ryder Cup get-together in Paris the week before we set off. I was at home that week, so I immediately started ringing round to see who could come. Lee Westwood and Darren Clarke were at home resting and Padraig Harrington, Sergio Garcia and

Jesper Parnevik were in America, but the others were all in Paris and immediately responded in the affirmative. In an informal atmosphere around the dinner table, we would be able to familiarise the players, especially the rookies, with what was likely to happen in Brookline and they would be able to ask questions and pick the brains of those who had already played a Ryder Cup and sampled the unique atmosphere of team golf's greatest competition. I thought it would be an additional boost for everybody if Seve could come along, and he graciously accepted.

Our time together at the Trianon Palace in Versailles was nothing short of brilliant. Get Seve on the subject of the Ryder Cup and you can listen to him talk all night, because he has been there and done everything in the A–Z of incidents and experiences. I would never criticise Seve because he has done so much for our game, but I think he found the Ryder Cup captaincy difficult throughout his year, particularly when having to deal with the press and the constant badgering for quotes and assessments. That might be the reason why he was not keen to do it again, and I can understand that. It is a huge job with constant demands, but the bottom line is that Seve wants to get his career back on track, and we in Europe, and I would like to think everywhere else, hope he does.

Although my job in Valderrama under Seve's captaincy was never clearly defined, it was never dull. I remember on the first night, with three full days to go before the start, six of us – me, Jane, Bernard and Lesley Gallacher and Ian and Glen Woosnam – were sitting having a drink at about eleven o'clock at night when Seve came in and said, 'Ian, I think you have had enough. You must go to bed.' Woosie, pretty sober by normal standards, was not all that happy, and replied, 'I'll just finish this one.' The door closed, but a few minutes later, by which time Woosie had got another half of beer, Seve returned and had another go. Woosie just said, 'I can't take this, I'm going to bed.' Seve was very strict on the discipline and drinking front. He made sure at the gala dinner that there was a limited amount of wine on each table: one carafe only, although Woosie did come to our table halfway through the meal to 'borrow' one of ours.

Seve is to a certain extent a man of extremes: he can do brilliant things one minute and the opposite the next. One thing which is constant is his presence, and he is without doubt one of the most inspirational people there has ever been in any sport, a huge figure in the team room whose contribution to the development of European golf has been immense. Seve can rub people up the wrong way by not talking to them enough or making them feel he is misjudging them, but it is not deliberate on his part. He is just very single-minded about doing the job his way.

In some ways it was a good job I was in Valderrama as an assistant because I knew the young guys well and could be of help to them. The captain has to dash around a heck of a lot because he has so many things to do, so the role of assistant has become extremely important. I know I was delighted to have Ken and Sam around because they took a lot of weight off my shoulders. That was something I tried to do for Seve: talking to the newcomers and making sure they understood what was going on, and maybe why they were not playing on the first day.

It must be remembered that Seve has a huge streak of brilliance running through him, and if he sees or senses something it is important to go with it. I will never forget asking before the first practice round on the Tuesday what he wanted me to do, figuring he would ask me to watch a few of our groups, chat to them and report back. He said, 'I want you to watch the

Americans.' I replied, 'What? Spy?' When Seve nodded his head, I told him that had I known, I would not have put on the team uniform that morning, but donned dark glasses and wig instead.

My surveillance instructions were simple: I had to watch how the Americans played the course; for instance, whether they could reach the par five seventeenth in two and, if they could, whether or not they were holding it with their approach shots. Seve told me that if he could do anything to the course which might take away any advantage they might have, he would.

As a spy, I would have made a damn good bus conductor. The American captain, Tom Kite, soon noticed me skulking around, so I popped under the ropes, went over to him on the ninth green and said hello. Tom said, 'What are you doing here?' and I replied, 'It's OK. Seve's sent me to spy on you.' I am usually taking the mickey most of the time, so Tom just laughed and did not believe me for one second. It must be said I was more Basildon Bond than James Bond. If my work produced any useful information it was of a very limited nature, and covered only the comings and goings on the seventeenth. Seve was not sure what to do about the green. The Americans generally hit higher with less spin, whereas our boys went in lower with more action on the ball. Their players were actually holding it better, so we sat for the best part of an hour debating the issue: should we soak it so everybody could hold it, or shave it so nobody could. We rolled balls off the front right of the green to see if they would trickle into the water. Seve even sent the last practice four back to the tee to play the hole again. We need not have worried. The decision was taken out of our hands by three inches of overnight rain.

One thing is always definite with Seve: he misses nothing. And it was that attention to detail and his fund of memories and stories I wanted to unlock when we sat down for dinner on the eve of the Lancôme Trophy. Nobody was disappointed. I had got the feeling when I first asked Seve to come to the dinner that he was a little unsure about the wisdom of it, which is why he agreed to come but warned that he might have to leave early. However, as soon as he started talking about the Ryder Cup, he enjoyed the evening as much as the guys enjoyed listening to him.

Seve and José Maria Olazábal bounced their experiences and anecdotes off each other and the newcomers got a taste of exactly what it would be like once the national anthems had been sung and the doors opened for the first day's play. They had to be prepared for it, or it could threaten to overwhelm them. I wanted nobody driving blind, because when you arrive at a Ryder Cup there always seems to be plenty of time because play does not start for four days, but players are rushed off their feet and the week goes by in a flash. It proved a very fruitful evening, and although it may not have been essential to the overall scheme of things, there were a few new boys there and it was definitely a no-lose tactic.

If a more passionate man about golf than Seve walks the world's fairways, I have yet to meet him. He even plays practice rounds as if the entire Spanish economy would collapse should he lose. When Howard Clark and I took on Seve and David Gilford in foursomes practice for the 1995 Ryder Cup at Oak Hill, we were only playing for ten dollars – enough for me because I do not like losing full stop – but it is not so much the money with Seve as the pride. He would have a sleepless night after a loss.

Gilly's chipping has been a source of amusement for those of us who have known him for some time, but Seve was not quite prepared for what he would witness when his partner stood over a little flop shot close to one green. After two long practice swings, when he brushed the grass and made everybody believe he knew what he was intending to do, the time came when he had to hit the ball. A deceleration at impact meant the ball popped forward no more than a foot, and Seve said, 'No, no, no. What you do?' before getting hold of Gilly's sand wedge and inspecting the bounce on the bottom of it. He then tossed the club on the ground, got out his own, stroked it lovingly across the sole, showed it to Gilly and smiled. 'This is what you need,' he said, before putting down a couple of balls and chipping them both to within six inches of the hole. Seve then watched in amazement as Gilly repeated his earlier shot and flopped it no more than a foot forward. Seve's face was a picture. He looked so confused; he just could not understand that Gilly could not do what he showed him.

That was not the last time Seve was shocked by Gilly at Oak Hill, and the second time was more important because it happened during the actual match. Seve and I were both in the clubhouse having a quick sandwich before going out to encourage the others when Gilly came to the eighteenth with his singles match against Brad Faxon in the balance. He had flown the green into a cleanish lie, but not on very nice ground. Gilly pulled out a six iron, and Seve could not believe it, watching him take a practice swing and groaning, 'No, no, no.' He put down his Coke and sandwich and headed out of the clubhouse at full speed to try to stop him, but it was too late. Fortunately it did not matter because Gilly managed to hang on for a win, but to this day Seve remains bemused by Gilly's chipping.

And when talking or thinking about Seve, I always recall this story. During the 1993 Ryder Cup at the Belfry, Costantino Rocca had a nightmare finish to his singles match and lost, so captain Bernard Gallacher asked Seve if he would go to the eighteenth, collect Costa and make sure he was all right. Seve went away, but fifteen minutes later Costa appeared on his own. 'Did Seve find you?' asked Bernard. 'Yes,' replied Costa. 'But I couldn't stop him crying.'

Back in Paris, a feeling of anticipation had gradually been building throughout Lancôme week. We were getting close, and it seemed a long time since I had accepted the captaincy. Suddenly the time came when the team was to assemble, ready to fly out and do battle, and I was really getting into it, my brain starting to go into overdrive. I had done as much groundwork as I could, and now it was about time to get over there and see how we could do.

We gathered at the Heathrow Hilton late on Sunday night, 19 September. Mark Watson, the tour's travel services manager, did a wonderful job to ensure that everything ran smoothly, because I wanted everything to be like clockwork with no hassle for the players. I wanted their minds on just one thing.

Unfortunately, my wife's mind had obviously been on other things. She had flown in from Leeds with her parents, John and Jeanne, and taken a car to the hotel. Five minutes after she checked in she realised she had left her travelling bag in the back of the car, which was now hurtling down the M4 to central London. The bag contained all the things she absolutely did not want to lose: jewellery, contact lenses, etc. In a search-and-find mission I am sure would have made spymaster Seve proud, Ryder Cup director Richard Hills, an indefatigable worker behind the scenes along with the PGA's Mike Gray, and Edward Kitson and Mark MacDiarmid from the tour, had the bag detected and returned within half an hour, much to Jane's relief (not to mention mine). We just had time to have a few drinks with

Jane's parents, John and Jeanne, and my parents, Jim and Bobbie (her name is Doreen, but everybody calls her Bobbie, and I have no idea why; I must ask one day) before turning in.

Check-in was between 7.30 a.m. and 9 a.m., but I told the players closer to nine would be fine as they were going to be up early for the next five days. Lee Westwood was a bit late and did not arrive until ten (those motorways again), but it did not matter because we did not walk through for another fifteen minutes.

Before long, everyone was ready to go. We had reached the stage where we were reading all the articles being written about the team, captain and assistants, and were collectively getting into Ryder Cup mode. Jacklin and Faldo had had their moans, but I do not think anybody in the press had much sympathy with them. I felt we had done some solid groundwork and were a well-balanced team, and we were quietly confident without being over-confident. You can always get your bottom spanked at whatever level of golf, so it is pointless saying you are going to win. I felt we were going to play well, and I left it at that.

I had spoken to the players about dealing with the press, and we felt that so far we were doing quite well on that front. I was particularly pleased by the coverage – we asked for a fair crack of the whip, and we got one – because I had had a somewhat chequered history with the guys from the Fourth Estate. In my early years on tour I was a rebel, I looked miserable, I was a bit of a pain, etc. but I did not mind it because to some extent it was true. I thought it amusing when people described me as bad-tempered and unhelpful. I actually enjoyed getting bad press then, but when you get older, as a husband and a committee member it tends to be a less pleasurable experience. So I tried very hard not to get into trouble.

I became more of a veteran in the mid-1980s and relationships with Fleet Street and the provinces were pretty normal, but for some unknown reason I had a couple of very bad experiences in 1989, and things soured. Richard Dodd, God rest his soul, gave me a couple of bad write-ups in the *Yorkshire Post*, and it made me extremely angry. There was no call for what he wrote; I did not like it, and felt it simply was not right.

Then I withdrew after two rounds of the Monte Carlo Open, even though I had made the cut. I realised the course was just not doing my game any good and I did not want to stay. I did not like the principality either. It was nothing but motorways and high-rise blocks, noisy and smelly and anything but enjoyable. I wanted to go home, so I did, and got slammed in the press for it. Someone wrote that I had stormed off the course, which could not have been further from the truth because I came off quite calmly having made my decision. What is more, I had not broken any rules and actually got paid last-place money, but that did not stop the boys in the press tent having a go.

I hated that kind of reporting, especially as it was inaccurate. I felt I had to take a stand against it, so when I found myself in the press room for interviews as our rules required, I started answering yes and no to questions and generally being unhelpful. The only information they got out of me were details of the round. It did not go down very well with them, but I thought I had given them a good run for their money over the years, and for somebody of my standard of play, they had had plenty of pages out of me. I felt I was getting a raw deal, and I still believe I was absolutely right to do what I did, even if it did sour relations for a while. I remember Dai Davies of the *Guardian* being particularly peeved, as were a number of others, but I was not in the least bit worried what they thought.

For a good few years there was an atmosphere of coolness because I did not trust them and they were not particularly enamoured with somebody who would not give them much information. Things reverted to normal eventually, but I still feel if you are treated badly then you have the right to react.

All I wanted from the press for the Ryder Cup was fair reporting, and that is what we got; the little criticism we received was all constructive. The reporting in Great Britain and Ireland was nothing less than I could have asked for in every respect. I knew that if I wanted fairness then I would have to reciprocate by being as accessible as possible. I do not know how far I succeeded in that, but I tried to be as available as possible and spent a lot of time talking to journalists. When Seve was captain, in Ryder Cup year he restricted his appearances at the press centre to one a month at one stage, but I always went in if asked. I felt it was the right thing to do, and it paid dividends. If I was going over to America at the helm of a team, I did not need to do it on the back of a load of bad publicity.

There were plenty of cameras flashing away as we made our way en masse through the airport, and the moment we started to walk I realised that this was it. We were now in the full glare of the Ryder Cup. Although nothing could have been potentially more aggravating than Jane losing her travel bag, there was another scare before we boarded Concorde, and I was prepared to delay its departure to overcome it.

José Maria Olazábal admitted to having a problem with his game: coach John Jacobs, an integral member of the tour party, had left his passport in Southampton. He had brought his wife's with him instead, which was a bit stupid because she is a helluva lot shorter and much prettier than he is. I certainly wanted John on the plane with us, so a dispatch rider was sent to fetch the missing document. Olly was unhappy, so the rest of the team were quite happy for us to wait if it meant he could have an extra session with his guru. Most of them were not that bothered about Monday practice anyway. The passport arrived just in time, and we were able to savour the atmosphere in the airport as people called out good luck messages and generally wished us well. It was a good feeling to know that people back home were willing us on to win.

Miguel and Darren went off looking for fast car magazines (between them they could probably set up their own Grand Prix outfit). Everyone did his own thing, but we were already feeling like a team. The only people missing were the guys who had been playing in the USA and Andrew Coltart's wife, Emma, who had recently given birth for the first time. It was a shame she could not be there because Emma would have had a whale of a time.

Team pictures were taken with the BA pilots in the Concorde Lounge, and the girls cracked open some champagne. One or two of them had gone eleven or twelve hours without a drink, so they were soon starting to get a little twitchy. Then we were on board and taking off. Apparently, we crossed in a record time for a commercial aircraft, but there was still plenty of time for somebody to have a crack at sinking the longest ever putt (I was immediately disqualified on grounds of inability). As it was a putting contest, it seemed only fair to give a Spaniard a shot at it. The unanimous nomination was Olly, and ten seconds after giving the ball a fair old whack towards the toilet at the back of the plane a new world record of something like four miles was ratified.

There was hardly much time for anything else, and there were no dramas this time, unlike our trip to

Kiawah in 1991. I went forward to the cockpit on this occasion to land us, or at least spectate; the only time I have seen so many dials was when I looked inside Miguel's Ferrari. It was fascinating coming into New York, where we had to land to refuel (or get Monty a hamburger, I cannot remember which). It had been David Gilford's turn to land us in Kiawah, and we seemed to be circling for a long time. Apparently they could not get the undercarriage down, so eventually they had to send somebody down into the bowels to wind it down with a spanner.

Like many other sportsmen, golfers get bombarded with requests for things to auction for charity, and when I have flown Concorde in the past I have always tried to get a menu signed to give away to a deserving cause. It would be easy to sign and send a golf glove, but that would probably have a hole in one of the fingers and fetch about £2.50, if somebody was feeling generous, so during Ryder Cups I have always tried to accumulate things like menus, shirts and jumpers, which people are very happy to accept and auction.

The nicest thing I was able to procure from this particular match was something of a captain's privilege: twenty prints from a limited edition of 1,000 paintings of the third hole at Brookline. The artist, Graham Baxter, brought them all up to sign. I have reasonably fast hands and a reasonably fluid, albeit unreadable, signature, so it only took one and a half hours, which beat Seve's time at Valderrama by about four days. Graham was also signing them, and he was about two-thirds of the way through when I noticed a faint line running through the pictures. I pointed it out, and I thought Graham was going to have a heart attack when he realised there was a fault in the paper. He had to get a load more, do them all again and re-sign them all later at Wentworth. At least our efforts were not in vain, because I got two signed at Brookline, one for myself and another for a friend's charity. It went for £1,500, so it was definitely worthwhile.

At least the menus did not take too long to sign, and before the ink was dry we were in Boston. I had been over the previous November with Jane to meet Ben and Julie Crenshaw and generally get my bearings in the city in terms of the hotel, course, etc. It is a remarkable place, and I remember it being a building site from airport to hotel, and thinking it would be no better come September. It was as if they were rebuilding the entire state of Massachusetts on a 500-year plan. Ben was there when we landed, at the end of the gangway ready to greet the team, along with a line of dignitaries. I have never seen the point in these large-scale receptions, because you say hello, shake hands and then move on. For me to remember anybody, I have to spend six weeks in their company. Anyway, we met the Mayor of Boston, the Mayor of Massachusetts, the Mayor of the Eastern Seaboard, the governor, the governor's daughter and the governor's second cousin (I think).

When we had landed in Kiawah there were thousands lining the edges of the runways, watching us land, and just as many waiting for us to come out of the airport. There was hardly anybody in Boston. They either could not get through the roadworks or were not that interested – probably the latter.

The first in a long series of press interviews followed. It was very well choreographed because we were told somebody would speak for eight seconds, then somebody else for one minute and 43 seconds. They like it perfectly planned in the USA, but the best-laid plans of mice and men did not take Ben Crenshaw into account. Timings tend to get cocked up when he sees a microphone; occasionally he gives the impression that he would be quite happy spending the whole day behind one. Anyway, we rattled off the usual platitudes and pleasantries, and then jumped on a bus, drove through the building site and soon arrived at the Four Seasons, our home for the week, and a very good one at that.

Boston is a fabulous city with a lot going for it. My first visits to America were confined to Los Angeles and Florida, which are not fabulous places and do not have as much to commend them. I thought everywhere in America, where anything older than three years is considered an antique, must be the same. Not so Boston, and definitely not the Four Seasons, where the entire fifth floor was at our disposal. The Americans were on the floor above, but apart from the odd bout of snoring we neither saw nor heard anything of them throughout the week.

At Oak Hill we had been on the same floor as the Americans, so this time round there was no chance of a repeat of an incident of four years earlier when Fred Couples wandered into our team room on the Thursday evening at about 9.30 p.m. The girls had had a couple of glasses of wine, which is unusual, because normally they do not drink at all (well, no more than a bottle of sherry before lunch), and when Fred came in things got a bit noisy. Fred was standing behind the door, and whenever it opened he would be completely hidden. The noise had reached its zenith when the door swung wide open, Fred jumped back against the wall and Sam Torrance came in. He had just gone to bed about twenty minutes earlier, and said, 'What's all the noise about? I'm trying to get some sleep.' Fred poked his head out, and said, 'Sorry, Sam, that's my fault.'

Everything we had asked for and needed at the Four Seasons was there. The food was awesome, and the staff were wonderfully helpful. The three tables I had also asked for were already in place. I did not want anything to stop the feeling of us being a team, and I thought three large tables would keep bunches of players together. We were the ones in the driving seat making the decisions, and I did not want to be seen in a corner all the time with Ken and Sam; we had to spread ourselves around. We would be a team without secrets, without cliques, free of inhibitions. I knew I was going to have to consult with my assistants quite a bit during the week, especially if there was a problem or a clash of personalities, but I did not want to be seen forever hugger-mugger with them. We had to split up as much as possible so that the players would feel everything was in the open. I have seen problems before when a captain persistently consults the same person in team areas; the others quickly get the feeling they are not in on the act. I did not want that thought even to enter my players' heads.

We also had a lounge area with three settees, a few chairs and a widescreen television. There was also a video room, so if there were any kids around and they wanted to watch *The Simpsons*, *Jungle Book* or *Debbie Does Dallas*, they could go in there.

We had nothing fixed for arrival day apart from a get-together and an early-evening team meeting. Most of the boys went up to the course to hit a few balls, play a few holes or simply familiarise themselves with Brookline Country Club. I think Monty decided against practice; he had picked up a callus the previous year and did not want to risk a recurrence, or further Harley Street bills.

Ken, Sam and I went for a stroll with our wives through the town. I went looking for a ski magazine, because if we were not doing too well during the match, I reckoned I might need something to read on my buggy. Sam and Suzanne were looking for new sunglasses, because I think they were down to their last thirty pairs. Several people called out to us, including plenty of Irish, who seemed to know who we were. Everybody was incredibly friendly, as most are in this part of the States, but, although we did not know it at the time, there is a small but significant minority who are not.

Having been to enough Ryder Cups to realise the rest of the week was going to be hectic, a quiet afternoon was definitely called for, so it was back for a lie down, a leisurely bath and then a team meeting in the other half of the captain's suite – a modest area with just four settees, an enormous dining table and a fridge forever being filled with beer. There were one or two doors I never had a chance to open, but they probably led to a swimming pool or a tennis court.

Europe's Class of '99 assembled at the appointed hour, and it proved a good opportunity for them to sign the prints, to air any questions they might have, and for me to impart any knowledge I had accumulated. I was also in a position to give them their first practice day pairings. Lee and Darren were together, playing with Monty and Paul; Miguel and José would play against Padraig and Jarmo; and Sergio and Jesper would take on Jean and Andrew. I felt it would be a good opportunity to test the likely pairings. If anybody did not like the course or was playing badly, then I would take it from there. I was prepared to be flexible, although as things developed during the week it might have seemed that I was totally inflexible. That was not the case. I was ready to switch at a moment's notice.

The meeting also gave me the opportunity to impress on them a few ground rules and guidelines. I needed to know if anybody was not happy in foursomes, because if you are not on your game in that discipline it can be a complete nightmare. They had to tell me immediately if they felt they needed a rest on the Saturday – a point I would check on regularly throughout the week. I wanted to be absolutely sure they were capable of five rounds in three days. Physically there should be no problem with this, but golf at this level of competition can be immensely draining, and a player may not always be the best judge of whether or not he is up for it. Having said that, the captain must have his opinion because it puts him in a better position to make an overall assessment. I also warned them to be ready for the greens to be cut lower, although as it turned out I do not think they were.

There was quite a bit of input from the players during my little run through the list of dos and don'ts; in fact, I was amazed by some of the things which start to run through a player's mind before an important competition. When the pressure mounts, a player gets increasingly nervous about aspects of the game such as dropping the ball and taking relief, and even wondering whether or not he is in the right for getting relief from a rabbit scrape. It is peculiar, but the worst thing that can happen in matchplay is to be penalised for breaking the rules, so if anybody had anything on his mind then the start of the week was definitely the right time to air it.

Andrew Coltart was starting to wonder if a couple of his grips were legal, because they had become worn through use and were not quite round any more. I did not think there was a problem with that, but I decided to contact John Paramor, the team's rules official and match referee, just to be on the safe side, and he was able to confirm that no rule had been broken. Someone else asked if you could touch the line of your putt with your putter head to remove loose impediments, and I was able to confirm that they could. Monty wondered if there was an out-of-bounds area to the left of the first hole. There is out-of-bounds forty yards left on that hole, and since Monty had not been that wild for thirteen years, I could only assume that he asked because he was getting a bit bored.

Of the points I tried to put across, none was more emphasised than this: if they had two putts to win a hole, they had to make sure they took them. I did not want anybody charging the first putt four feet past, because when the Ryder Cup heat is turned up putts of that length seem immeasurably longer. It was a message I put across all week; I never tired of saying it, although the players quickly tired of hearing it. By the end of the week any mention of it was greeted with a deafening chorus of boos and derision.

I also reminded them that if anybody was practising on the course during Friday and Saturday then they had to keep a two-hole gap between them and the last match. Of those playing, they had to be aware that if the side was three down or more in three matches then there had to be no surrender, because if they kept up the pressure then there was a chance that at least one of the matches would emerge with half a point, and that could be vital in the final analysis. I felt it essential that they realised a match could change in an instant. They probably already knew it, but there was no harm in drumming it home. At least if I was saying these things then they knew I was definitely thinking about the match, not just swanning around having a glass of beer in the clubhouse.

I also told them not to take any notice if their opponents did not appear to be nervous, because they would be. In fact, they would be every bit as nervous as us, and if they were kept under pressure in front of their home crowd they would more than likely crack at some stage. 'Get the best out of your own game and just keep going at them' was my message. The team kit did not include white towels. They were also not to be frightened of clubbing down off the tee. It was a point which would not be all that relevant because the course never really dried out, but there was some significance to it, because if you are the first to hit to the green in matchplay you can put a reasonable amount of pressure on.

I also warned the players not to respond to aggressive celebrations, either by their opponents or by people in the crowd. I told them we would have enough of our own supporters there, and I was expecting, as in 1995 at Oak Hill, that the crowd would be extremely fair. I told them to make friends with the crowd if they could, to chat to them during practice rounds and generally have a bit of banter, give balls away, sign autographs and smile a lot. I stressed the importance of not letting the crowd turn against them, and I felt we did everything in our power to prevent that happening, but unfortunately that attempt would be in vain. I genuinely wanted the Americans to like us, and I thought it would not be difficult because we had a lot of personalities in the team. Unfortunately, Brookline is not Oak Hill.

With regard to coaches, I told the players that during play everything had to be done through the captain, that there should be no direct contact. I thought this would prove unlikely, but events proved me wrong again.

I also reminded them that after two days at a snail's pace playing foursomes and fourballs on Friday and Saturday, Sunday's play would be faster. It can be a difficult transition to make, so I told the caddies to remember this as well, so they could put the reins on if necessary.

Altercations had to be avoided at all costs. I felt any arguments would probably be resolved in favour of the home side, because the minute you have any sort of problem supporters will start liking their own players more and the opposition less. Because our followers would be in a minority, it was therefore not a good idea to get involved in any form of confrontation. If it did happen, then they had to take their time, keep playing and call me so I could come over and sort it out.

If, for instance, their opponent was practice-putting at length after completion of a hole, then they should not let it annoy them. This is something which started a few years ago and can go on for a long time; some players try to use it to disrupt their opponents' rhythm. I had already mentioned to our PGA that maybe there should be some sort of restriction placed on practice-putting, but the US PGA declined the offer. My fears that it would cause trouble did bear fruit.

Prince Andrew is a great supporter of our side, and I reminded the players that he might be wandering in and out of the team room. His Royal Highness does not make a nuisance of himself; he just pops in, has a drink and then disappears. There is no problem with that, but if there were other people unconnected with the team in there and somebody had a problem with it, then the player with the beef had to come to me. We had no problems in this area until the Sunday night, when Monty made his feelings absolutely clear that he wanted somebody thrown out. And that was fine: I told the players repeatedly that anything I, Ken or Sam could do, no matter how trivial, then all they had to do was ask. Similarly, the wives should go to Jane, Suzanne or Dawn.

Dave Cannon of Allsport was the official team photographer, and he would be wandering around now and again in the team room, at the course and in the hotel. I said I did not think he would be a nuisance, and reminded the players that it was always nice to have an album of pictures at the end of the week. I also informed them that Derrick Cooper, a tour colleague and member of the board of directors, would be my on-course chauffeur. Brookline is such a tricky course to get around, and sometimes you need to get somewhere a bit faster by buggy. For me, having somebody to put the buggy in position was ideal, and Coops was a wonderful traffic cop, an absolute master of the art. I asked the players' permission for him to come in the team room at the course every now and then so he could get something to eat, and no one had a problem with that – all the guys know him and he is a good laugh. Similarly, while Sam was happy to negotiate the gridlock on his own, Phil 'Wobbly' Morbey, Ian Woosnam's caddie, had come over to perform similar duties for Ken. (If you have ever seen Wobbly run, you will understand the origin of his nickname. He is like a *Thunderbirds* puppet with dodgy joints. I also have something of a gait which has provoked comment over the years, very little of it favourable, but unlike Wobbly I have an excuse: I grew up on a course with 50,000 sheep on it, and if you did not lean forward and look down it was off to the dry cleaner's every five minutes.)

Because I did not want anybody kept in the dark, I told the players they would be informed as soon as possible if they were playing in the next series of matches, but at the same time to be aware that sometimes decisions had to be made either late or on the spur of the moment, and that if I had not had time to tell them for whatever then they should try to understand it was not because they had been overlooked. I reminded them that it was the team result that counted at the end of the day, and that four people had to be left out of every series. Ryder Cups are very unpredictable; you only need a couple of players to have a bad round or two and all your plans can change.

That is why I stressed the importance of being flexible, so that whoever they were paired with they made sure as far as possible they were comfortable with and would be able to go out and perform. Preparation for the foursomes had to include being aware as soon as possible whether they wanted to tee off on the odd or even holes, so that if they were put into a new practice pairing they would know immediately who would be teeing off.

My advice when practising and actually playing foursomes was for them to keep swinging and loosening up so that they would be ready for the next shot. Sometimes you can go a couple of holes and feel you have hardly hit the ball, and it is surprising how quickly everything can stiffen up.

Many of the things I told the players that evening may have seemed obvious, but my rule throughout had been never to leave anything to chance, and I would touch on all these topics every now and then throughout the week. This Monday-night session was a long one because I had a lot of things to say; later in the week, when everyone has been playing and practising all day, no one wants a team meeting that lasts forty minutes. About ten is ideal, so that you can have your bath, food, massage and hang upside down from the ceiling or whatever you want to do during the evening.

So now they all knew how things were going to be, what I wanted from them and what they could expect from me. Above all else, as I said, I wanted them to know that I was thinking all the time about how we were going to win the Ryder Cup, and everything had to be in the open so that if there was a problem it was easy to come straight to us with it. There would be no curfews and no ban on alcohol that week; a good few of the team rarely drank anyway. I was dealing with adults, and they knew what to do, what was best for their games. My job was simply to ensure that mentally they were OK, in the right pairings and looked after properly by all and sundry.

Everybody seemed to be happy, settled and ready. Unfortunately this was on Monday night, and there were still three full days to go before start of play.

7 Boston Tee Party

THERE WAS A DEFINITE BUZZ in the team room and a feeling of expectancy on the course as we started the first serious practice session on Tuesday morning. I was not needed to hold their hands or cut their fruit at breakfast, and I could see no reason to practise captaincy while they practised golf, so for me it was a leisurely start to a busy day.

My first real contact with the players was on the first tee, and the first thing that hit me was how well everybody was playing, with the possible exception of Olly. No surprise there, because he occasionally says he is not in good form when actually he is hitting a six iron four feet from where he would like to. But I was more than happy with everyone else, although the last thing I wanted was for them to peak too soon. My reservations were calmed by the knowledge that if somebody is in form on the first day of practice he will usually carry it through the week, even though Ryder Cup weeks are much longer than normal. In Europe, a lot of the guys, including me, will arrive at a venue at the earliest on the Tuesday evening, and just as often Wednesday morning for a Thursday start. Ryder Cup week is an arrive-Monday-start-Friday week – a long time, and probably the reason why we only play nine holes on the last day of practice.

I watched each of the three groups for six holes, starting off with Lee and Darren, and Monty and Paul.

Had they all been playing well I had already decided they would be in the starting line-up, and they were. I then dropped back to pick up Olly and Mechanico, Padraig and Jarmo. In the space of just six or seven holes there was a possibility I would not see the full picture, so I had asked Ken to accompany them all the way round so that he could assess Olly's driving. Our fears were confirmed, but it was still early days. Sam went out with Sergio and Jesper, and Andrew and Jean, and cast his educated eye over them.

The early signs were very encouraging, particularly from Padraig, who had had those two late second-place finishes to make the team and was carrying his form forward, and also Mechanico, who was absolutely ripping it. The two of them looked tremendously impressive even at that stage of the week, and both looked as if they were enjoying the course. If Olly did not fancy the foursomes then I had his deputy already waiting to team up with Mechanico.

Practice could not have gone more smoothly, and after the round came the daily visit to the press tent. I had originally been scheduled for interview while the players were still out on the course, but I got that changed. It does not matter if I disappear when the players are on the practice range because I am not going to give them a lesson, but while they are on the course I feel I should be there. The more time I spend with them the more I know what they are thinking and what makes them tick. Things might slip out; I might become aware of something which might be important.

I had asked the team to make themselves popular with the crowd and the press, and I wanted to do that too, so when I went into the interview area my only objective was to be honest, polite and my normal self. I knew the last of these might cause problems, especially in America where irony tends to fly over heads at

Concorde height, and I was aware my brand of humour might not be instantly acceptable because you get the impression with Americans that they either take everything you say literally or fail to notice from which direction you are coming. But, just as I had tried to answer whatever the European press had asked, similarly I wanted the American writers on board. If they were not going to make us favourites, I certainly did not want them calling us anything unpleasant.

Their questioning was of a form I had come to expect, and their acceptance of my answers equally so. If you make a scathing remark to a British journalist, there is a good chance you will get a tart response, and quite rightly so. In the USA, they tend to put down their pens and wonder what is going on. Their players are so incredibly polite to the press, it is way over the top. Some interviews get so sycophantic you just want to reach for the sick bag. It is farcical. I believe you can have a decent relationship with journalists without creeping around them with your tongue hanging out.

Actually, my only problem with the press conferences in Boston was that there were so many spotlights trained on the stage I was never sure whether I was facing the world's press or a live theatre audience. I did hear a few laughs occasionally, but not much clapping, so I always assumed it must have been the press. And although honesty was my only policy, for some unknown reason the Americans did find me mildly entertaining.

I definitely did not want to alienate anybody, so I tried not to look dismissive if the questioning bordered on the boring or repetitive. I told them the course was in stunningly good shape and faultlessly set up, in the way that it should be. If a player was in form I guessed he would return 65, but if he was in bad shape then it might be more like 74. What I did not tell them, of course, was that Ben Crenshaw had definitely engineered the course to suit the Americans. Now that is not a criticism, nor is it bad sportsmanship, just something a captain must do in his own side's interests. Seve tried to do it at Valderrama: he was constantly looking for ways to doctor the course to give us an edge. If you can present a course which gives your side an advantage then well and good, and I am sure the Belfry in 2001 will be tailored to Sam Torrance's requirements. Ben obviously believed that on the whole he had a team which could hit the ball a long way, and with Woods, Duval, Love and Mickelson he was right. Even if their tee shots found the rough they would still be able to reach the green with their approach shots, whereas some of ours might struggle.

The Americans were very interested in my strategy for deciding pairings and I told them I looked for players who would gel together, understand each other and preferably speak the same language. In foursomes I would look for players who did not make mistakes, whereas in fourballs the odd error was acceptable, as long as it came on the back of a few birdies.

But it was not long before the first bouncer was bowled by a British journalist. Our boys do love a sniff of controversy, and Jeff Maggert had offered them an easy opening by saying earlier in the day that the American team had the twelve best golfers in the world in it. 'Have they?' I replied. 'I've always said the world rankings are wrong, and I'm glad Jeff agrees with me.' I know they were hoping I might bite a bit deeper than that, but by this time I had been up quite a few hours and was hardly likely to fall for something quite so obvious.

Then the Americans tried a curve ball of their own, wondering if I had had words with Ben about David Duval and Tiger Woods overtaking our boys in practice by jumping from hole eight to fifteen after catching up with them. I had no idea it had happened, and would not have minded in the slightest had I known, because such a practice used to be commonplace, so I parried that one easily enough too.

I noticed the Spanish press had their pens cocked the moment I was asked what contribution their country-men had made to the European effort over the years. As I said, I was not looking to score points anywhere, so I simply replied, 'Seve was a big inspiration. He brought a unique passion to the matches and his partnership with Olazábal has been instrumental in the results we have enjoyed. And now we regard Sergio García as a young Seve, although he is his own man and player.'

Previous experiences had taught me several lessons about dealing with the press – not least how to spot a question with a bullet in it. At one stage they wanted to know what I thought of former Ryder Cup player Brian Barnes' belief that the rivalry had become almost Third World War in its intensity. I said that I thought that was overstating things because a lot of my players had friends in the American side and vice versa. 'It's serious golf because we're both out here to win, but at the end of the week I'll be able to shake Ben warmly by the throat and we'll sit down and have a beer.' The comment was received well; its irony would only develop later.

The press do seem obsessed with rivalries, and somewhere along the line I knew I would be asked to compare Tiger and Sergio. I felt that because they were hitting the ball off the middle of the club virtually every shot then their powers of recovery were much greater than the normal player. They also added charisma to the game, and were both massive talents. Tiger was the game's dominant force, but Sergio would be among those challenging him in the years to come.

The Americans were similarly engrossed in discove-ring which team was the hungrier. One look in our team room would have convinced them that my players were every bit as good with a knife and fork in their hands as a driver or eight iron, but I guess the questioner was more interested in a different kind of appetite. 'It's very easy if you lose a match to blame it on not being hungry enough, having a bad captain or the players not being team-orientated,' I said, 'but that's looking for excuses because it comes down to how they play. I think sometimes the roles of captain and team spirit can be overstated, and if you look for excuses you are hiding the fact that one team played slightly better.'

I had touched on the captaincy, and it was seized upon quickly. 'What makes a good captain?' I was asked. 'A good team,' I replied, knowing that I would be pushed for more. 'And what would be the role of a captain on a good team?' they came back. I said the captain could make mistakes, but they were usually only obvious with hindsight. If the team played well, got on well together and had a decent team spirit, then being captain was a relatively easy job; if the players argued, were not happy, were in an uncomfortable hotel and were not getting the right food, there could be problems. We had no such problems. People found it somewhat surprising that I should consider the roll of the ball and a bit of good golf here and there capable of tipping the balance rather than the role of the captain, but that has been my firm belief for some time, because in terms of ability the gap between the teams is extremely narrow, and has been for quite some time.

Quite a few also wondered if our chances had been improved by the match being played on a more traditional layout like Brookline rather than a TPC, which has a more modern design and occasionally contains as much water as Lake Michigan. But at this level the course does not have a significant effect because, as Seve Ballesteros once said, 'Top golfers have to be able to play on any course, sleep in any bed and eat from any table.' I went on: 'It's easy to start second-guessing what might happen with courses, and also what your opponents might do with regard to pairings, but you can shoot yourself in the foot trying to work out what's going to happen.' I was asked whether a more experienced team had an advantage, and I had to admit that, ideally, a captain would prefer an experienced team, but there was absolutely nothing to be gained from having an experienced team if its members were not playing well. It was essential to have a good balance, and quick learners among the rookies.

But it was not long before we were back on the blood-and-guts questions (sometimes I wonder if journalists think golfers should be carrying machetes instead of mashies). One journalist, having spoken of it as a gentleman's game with both sides respecting each other, asked, 'Amid all that, is there still room for bloodthirsty competition in this event?' I tried to be as diplomatic as I could while wondering which planet he was visiting from. 'I don't think golf ever gets that serious,' I said. 'You give a hundred per cent and it means a lot to the players whether you win or lose the match, and to get into the team is an enormous honour and it matters, but people are not dying because of it. Whoever wins or loses, they will get over it. It's serious, but it's golf.'

And then we went on to questions about the crowd and how home-orientated they were likely to be. I said that after Kiawah in 1991 the team captains of 1993, Bernard Gallacher and Tom Watson, had done a great job calming the crowd situation, and since then the atmosphere had been good. In 1995 the galleries at Oak

Hill were absolutely brilliant – a fun crowd who loved a bit of banter and appreciated good golf. 'I have no reasons to suppose it will be any different this time,' I said, 'and I hope I'm not proved wrong.'

We had very little time after this friendly interrogation ended to get back to the hotel and prepare for that evening's welcome dinner. For the last nine years I have never been able to go to these occasions without fearing we might get a repeat of an embarrassing episode in Kiawah Island. Over the last decade, a religious fervour seems to have hit American golfers, and they cannot win a tournament without thanking the Almighty. The clergyman in Kiawah capped everything by including in his grace a prayer for both teams, but asking if God could look after the American team more. I could not believe what I was hearing, and it was most definitely not said in jest. If there is a God, I just could not see him taking a beer out of the fridge, putting his feet up and taking a serious interest in the outcome of a golf tournament; surely he would have more important things to do. I may be cynical in this respect (maybe God is a huge golf fan), but the way some of their players feel God is very much on their side, maybe they should be handicapped a couple of shots for having an extra caddie or calling on an outside agency.

It was at that dinner in 1991, too, that a film was shown of all the great shots from Ryder Cups down the years. I could not believe that of all the thousands of great plays only one from a European was considered worthy of inclusion. We have always known they were insular, but they certainly excelled themselves there.

This time the occasion was far more acceptable, and even after all our hurried preparations, we still managed to get there before the Americans. We were milling around having a beer when in they walked –

and what a sight! Fashion trends in America always seem to be four or five years behind ours, and the general consensus that evening was that they were quite welcome to their striped suits, blue shirts with white collars, and a tie which clashed spectacularly. The only thing missing from the outfit was a violin case.

Fashion explosions have happened before at Ryder Cups, but about the only time the two sides seemed to be in harmony was in the mid-1970s when we all wore Tom Watson-type flared trousers, and were very proud of them. It is amusing to look back, see all those Rupert Bear checks, and think, 'What on earth were you doing winning all those Opens wearing trousers like that?' Then you see pictures of yourself and we were all wearing them, although they probably did not fit as well as Tom's.

The Americans' late arrival for the welcome dinner meant we were running behind schedule. It was no big deal for us, but we thought our normally to-the-minute hosts would be thrown out of kilter because we knew they always liked to be in bed by ten past nine. I have no idea why that is, or what they do for so long while they are in bed; the fact remains they do like to retire early. Julie Crenshaw was extremely worried that the whole thing was behind schedule, that her husband's team would suffer through missing fifteen minutes' sleep. Maybe they are a sensitive bunch of lads, but Julie was ringing the kitchen every two minutes to check what was happening, and we were out of there the moment we had finished our dessert and before the coffee had percolated.

There was only just enough time for both captains to make a little speech. It was the one thing I was looking forward to least, because I just do not do after-dinner speaking. I am very relaxed being interviewed on television or in the press room, but standing up to speak in public is something I have always hated. At a tournament it is not too difficult, because you thank the crowd, the sponsors, the greenkeeper, the nanny, God (if you are American), etc., but standing up at the welcome dinner to say a few words filled me with terror – and it was only the first speech of many. Ben said a few words first (or quite a few in his case), and showed us the beautiful glass vase we were all getting as a present. Then it was my turn. Richard Hills had kindly written out the bare bones for me; I just personalised it.

It started well, because I opened by saying, 'I won't keep you long because we have got to get back so that Sergio can do his homework.' That went down well, but after that it was all wrong. I just could not get the words out, and I think I broke the world record for spluttering and stuttering. It was not good, but at least I never once said 'Golf will be the winner'. It has been said so many times it has given clichés a bad name, and every time I hear it I want to curl up and switch the television off. It had been my first foray into the world of public speaking, and I just about got away with it – but only just. At least it gave the team something to laugh at, and we had plenty of players high in the world rankings at heckling.

I survived the ordeal, and we were back at our hotel before we had time to say 'cappuccino', wondering what on earth had happened. In Europe we have a meal and then sit around for seven hours putting the world to rights and hoping that some of the foreign food we have just eaten will eventually digest (at Valderrama the Americans sent out for burgers and pizzas because they were unable to cope with the local fare). As it was Tuesday, a few of us went into the team room and had one more beer for the stairs, before people slowly wended their way to bed. Ken, Sam and I with Dawn, Suzanne and Jane were invariably the last to retire, and we were all of the same opinion: so far, so good.

Come breakfast on Wednesday, the team's eating habits were making themselves known. We had sent somebody out to get olive oil for Mechanico, because he was rather partial to a cereal bowl of boiled eggs swimming in a one-inch pool of the stuff. There was a contented look on his face as he tucked in. Another happy bunny was Jarmo, who ordered off the menu and got his dream breakfast for the first time: a gigantic bowl of pasta with lumps of chicken in it (the only things missing were the feathers) smothered in tomato sauce. He downed the lot, and two and a half hours later he was asking for a sandwich to be sent out on to the course. He must have hollow legs, because he only has a 24-inch waist and I had absolutely no idea where he was putting it.

Apart from Jarmo, nobody made that big a deal about breakfast, most people coming in and out at a fair rate of knots and several players opting to have it at the course, leaving early to avoid the traffic. The atmosphere was encouraging, the team got on well together, and everybody was relaxed and starting to enjoy the week. The apprehension was still there, but at least they felt everything was in place: the hotel was faultless, the course good, and they had everything they needed to be able to perform. Even if it is just a little thing, the last thing you want is somebody saying 'this is wrong, that's wrong', but nobody did because we really had no problems.

The facility of getting to know people better is at its height during Ryder Cup week, and I felt the team had bonded very quickly indeed. Without exception, the players had a great sense of humour and the team room was a happy place to be. The lack of egos was also a huge help, but a lot of the credit had to go to a very good behind-the-scenes team from the tour and PGA in Richard Hills, Mike Gray, Edward Kitson, Mark Mac-Diarmid and Mitchell Platts. Nobody was getting in the way of anybody else, and that is very important in Ryder Cup week. There had been no arguments, and Ken, Sam and I were not aware of any bad feelings. Ken and Sam would definitely have got wind if anything was amiss because that was one of the reasons they were there.

Basically, what Jane and I set out to achieve was to get the maximum number of points possible and for the team to enjoy the week. I felt we had made a good start in that direction. The guys had played well on Tuesday and were relaxed and settled. I had asked for slightly later tee times on Wednesday because I knew they would have acclimatised a bit more, having been awake and up at the crack of dawn the previous day. Monty and Paul went out first, because Monty's happiest flying round in two and a half hours, with Jarmo and Jean alongside them. Mechanico and Olly accompanied Darren and Andrew, while I put Lee and Padraig together with Jesper and Sergio. The spies from the press tent probably wondered why I had split up Lee and Darren, but this had nothing to do with subterfuge, it was simply a question of common sense. They are such good friends and spend so much time together I felt a change of scenery might benefit both for a day. A few switches here and there also helped in terms of flexibility, in case somebody intended for the opening series started to play badly and had to be replaced.

Most players had kept the form they took to Boston, so for me, as usual, it was just a question of keeping tabs and making sure everybody was happy and wanted for nothing. Our gut feelings about Paul continued to look very sound indeed, and he seemed to be perfectly at ease playing alongside Monty. He was focused and relaxed, and above all he seemed to belong. Since Carnoustie he has looked like an Open champion, which is not easy to do, and he cut an impressive figure on the Brookline fairways. In fact he was loving it out there with Monty, who in turn had found a partner he was happy with. They both play reasonably quickly, and their games are similar enough to gel well.

Playing for a few dollars tends to give practice an extra edge, and there was no shortage of bets. When I played in the Ryder Cup, I was never happy playing for more than ten dollars, but these boys were playing for hundreds, which would have frightened the hell out of me, but they were coping with it stoically. Everybody was happy, particularly Paul, who appeared to be collecting most of the money, along with Monty.

The only question mark still hung over Olly and his driving, although there was still plenty of time to find a cure for his ills. Just about every handicap golfer in Britain and Ireland would love to have the Spaniard's problems, but he had not won two Augusta green blazers without searching for perfection, and his voyage of discovery was continuing for the moment. The journey was not without its lighter side, as he proved during the back nine when the pairings changed from fourballs to foursomes. Olly put Mechanico in the trees off the thirteenth tee and he had a tricky shot to recover, having to bend the ball round some woodwork and over a lake to the green. Andrew Coltart, standing in the middle of the fairway, looked at the options and said to Olly, 'Has your man got the balls for this shot?' Olly had no doubts about his partner's form. 'Of course. Mechanico has the balls of an elephant,' he replied. The ensuing shot went a long way towards confirming his observation.

Olly had been spending five hours a day on the range with John Jacobs. I had seen less of him and

Mechanico than any other pairing, but that was deliberate, not an oversight. I did not want to put any
pressure on Olly or make him feel I was watching every
tee shot, while Miguel has been such a good player for
a long time that he did not need me there telling him
to relax.

The atmosphere between player and coach is occasionally fraught, and I imagine John's ears took a bit of
a battering as Olly's frustration set in, but there is
nothing unusual in that. If you are not giving and
taking, just standing there and listening, I am not sure
you are getting the best out of a relationship. My own
swing guru, Gavin Christie (he's called Rhino because
he is thick-skinned and charges a lot), has felt the
rougher edge of my tongue on occasion. When I am
having problems, he says, 'You're swinging well,' to
which I normally reply, 'How can I be swinging well
when I can't keep it on the planet?' Those of us who are
fairly technical always feel that if we are not playing
well there must be something wrong with the swing. It
is horses for courses, because although I cannot go out
without something to think about, Sam will not see his
coach before he starts play and will have no swing
thoughts when he gets to the first tee. For some it is not
impossible to have a swing thought at address, another
at takeaway, a third at the top and a fourth coming
down, so I can understand where somebody like Nick
Faldo is coming from. I am somewhat like that,
although people might not think it when they watch me
swing. Gavin was professional at Burley Park when I
started playing, and he set me off with the swing I have
today, so I hold him entirely responsible.

If Olly was struggling to make the foursomes combinations, then his deputy had already identified himself.
In tourspeak, Padraig was 'purring it' in practice –
hitting the ball a long way and dead straight. The form

he had shown getting into the team was continuing, and he was completely focused. (When Seve was captain in 1997, the one thing he kept telling the team was 'Focus, focus', but his pronunciation gave the word an entirely different slant. It was hilarious.)

I wanted to kick off with the strongest possible eight on Friday morning, because when a team gets off to a bad start in the USA and the home players and crowd really get into it, you can be trampled underfoot. I intended going for Monty and Paul, Sergio and Jesper, Lee and Darren, and Mechanico and Olly/Harrington.

Everybody knew the way I was thinking, although I imagine they all probably felt they would get a game before Sunday. We would start with numbers one to eight, and a player would come in if or when anybody needed a rest or maybe went off colour slightly. That was the way I saw it, but not the way it turned out, which was a great shame.

The captaincy issue seemed to be one which the Americans were keen for me to expand on at the Wednesday press conference, although I could not think why. I told them I was getting by, but it had been difficult zooming around on the buggy because the drizzle secmed always to get under the umbrella. Most of them seemed to know where I was coming from, but you can never be too sure. Irony was still not travelling too well east to west.

There was more of my tongue in my cheek when I told them the job had been plain sailing, but I was totally serious when I said I had a great bunch of lads with no egos, good assistants and a solid support structure. I was asked if I was surprised how loose my players were. Not at all, and in one respect they could expect to be extremely loose on Friday morning, but they were a relaxed bunch without mental problems and were both adaptable and flexible.

I then had to explain the French psyche to a questioner who appeared to believe that after what happened to Jean Van de Velde at the Open, he might be susceptible to pressure. 'I have no qualms about Jean,' I said. 'For seventy-one holes of that Open he was absolutely fantastic, hadn't put a foot wrong and played magnificently under pressure. The last hole? Well, when the French go down, they go down in flames.' The questioning naturally drifted on to Paul Lawrie, and I was able to assure them that here was a player destined for high places, the possessor of a short game only evident in the very top players. 'He has all the attributes a top player needs,' I said. 'I think the Open was one of the first examples of us seeing them all gel together. Paul is going to be around for quite a long time.'

I was asked what my strategy for playing the course would be, and I said I would start playing fairways/greens and then, as the game developed, weigh up the risk on each shot depending on the state of play, but there would be no way I would be in my players' faces because they all knew their way around a golf course and did not need me telling them how to play it. Although a US Open course, Brookline was set up much better and fairer than it would have been for a major.

If anybody needs motivating for the Ryder Cup these days they should not be playing in it, but it was a question which came up more than once. 'It's just not a problem,' I assured the scrum. 'I've got to de-motivate them so their heads don't explode. They want it badly; they want to do well; they want to win points; and they want to be the next Ryder Cup superstars.'

I was hoping that might settle that one, but sometimes it goes in one ear and does not hang around long before it is out the other. Nobody to date had tried to get me to make a prediction – not that I would have

anyway, apart from thinking it would be very close –
but the last question of the day threw up the chance for
the spin merchants to get to work if I was not too
careful. 'With a lot of talk about the Americans being
such heavy favourites, what argument would you give
as to why the Europeans will retain the Cup?' It called
for a straight bat. 'I've never said that we will retain the
Cup,' I replied. 'I'm perfectly willing to accept that
there's a possibility of any result in this match. I'm not
going to beat drums about how we are going to win. I
think we have a good team playing pretty well and I
think they will be hard to beat. The last six matches
have been very close, and a few rolls of the ball here,
a rub of the green there and a bit of luck in the middle
and the match can go either way. So I would not say we
are going to definitely do anything. You always have to
be aware of that element called luck.'

Luck or not, I certainly liked the way we looked,
and, with the exception of Olly, in his own estimation
at least, there was little to be sorted out as we headed
back to the hotel in readiness for that evening's gala
dinner. The players were all ready and eager for the
match to start, but there were still 36 hours to go, and
several of those would be spent in courtesy cars,
because a twenty-minute journey to the course could
take over an hour. The drivers, some of whom were
strangers to the area, oddly enough, had been told to
stick to a certain route, and this was proving a big
mistake. We were beginning to question the validity of
those plans, and to wonder if it was taking the Americans that length of time to reach the course.

The schedule was running a little bit tight, so I
changed the time to meet in the team room, and after
a few photographs with the girls, all of them with their
best frocks on and looking truly stunning, we made our
way to the dinner at the Boston Symphony Hall. There

was just time for a swift beer as we milled around saying hello to our counterparts, who had not come kitted out as gangsters this time. They had dressed more in a European style and looked extremely smart, probably because it was a black-tie evening. I lined up alongside Ben and we all walked in with our wives or partners to take our seats. I made sure Ken, Sam and I were at different tables so that we could keep our ears to the ground, just in case anybody had an ingrowing toenail or split ends, which is something I tend to suffer from.

When the main course arrived, Monty was not happy. To say the lamb was raw is an understatement because, as Jane said at the time, a good vet could have had it back on its feet and gambolling in the fields in no time. I swapped with Monty because I do not mind my meat still twitching. We had just started tucking in when the upper balcony started filling up with hundreds of people, there to watch the show. Half of them seemed to have binoculars, and suddenly we had an audience of 3,000 watching us getting to grips with the lamb chops. It was a bit unnerving, because Yorkshiremen normally pick the things up and give them a damn good chew. It was a pleasure best forgone on this occasion.

The teams were introduced by multi-sports-Emmy-award-winning television announcer Dick Enberg, who, on the basis of his performance that evening, would not have won any award apart from a wooden spoon. He had not been briefed adequately, if at all. He introduced Eimear Montgomerie as Elmear, which of course stuck for the week, and Laurae Westwood as Laura, and forgot Jarmo Sandelin and his wife completely. We shouted out to him, but he could not hear, so I wandered up on to the stage and introduced Jarmo and Linda myself because I thought it was the only way we were ever going to get over the hiccup. He then introduced the Americans and forgot all about Steve Pate's wife. I do not know who his researchers were, but they are now probably alternatively employed.

It was an enormous relief not to have to make a speech; after the welcome dinner débâcle I felt I needed a day and a half to prepare myself for the opening ceremony. I was able to sit back and enjoy the evening's entertainment, which was nothing short of five-star. Although I am not a classical music fan, the Boston Pops were absolutely fantastic. They even included some Elvis – Presley, not Costello – which was right up my street. I took an instant dislike to the conductor though, with his slightly foppish haircut in the Hugh Grant style, waving his baton around like a demented scarecrow, but by the end of the show I was a big fan. And if he and his orchestra were outstanding, Celine Dion was awesome. She lives next door to Jesper and said hello to him from the stage, pointing out that they both lived in Jupiter, Florida. A couple of us on adjoining tables shouted out simultaneously, 'In Jesper's case, that's just Jupiter.'

The entire evening was a huge success, and all credit to Ben and Julie, but it was now after ten o'clock – a late night for them, and getting towards the American team's tucking-in time, although none had turned into a pumpkin. For some reason, Ben, Jeff Maggert and Mark O'Meara ended up on our bus, which provided us with the opportunity for a little light relief. The team started belting out 'Jesse is our captain' to a tune I did not recognise, and when they finished I shouted out, 'Don't sing, just throw me the money,' to which Sam replied in an equally loud voice, 'Don't mention the money.' The comment was lost on nobody, particularly the three American poker faces at the back of the bus, although I am sure Jeff Maggert enjoyed Sam's aside a little more than he was prepared to show, given that he was sandwiched between two of the central figures in the Ryder Cup pay-for-play controversy.

The row had grown over a few years, but advocating representing your country for a few dollars more was destined to be a no-win situation. The general public could see players like Mark O'Meara, who had the highest profile in the pro-pay camp, making vast amounts of money and still complaining he was not getting a bit more for representing his country. Somebody earning an average wage and working very hard for it must have found the situation incomprehensible, if not offensive, and I had to agree. The whole thing was absolute madness.

In my opinion, it is ridiculous and obscene to want to be paid for playing in the Ryder Cup. You could make some kind of a case for payment in some competitions played under the flag, but the Ryder Cup is the ultimate team event in our sport and there are many players on both sides of the Atlantic who would willingly pay money to play in it. It is inconceivable that people should want to receive a large wad, and that feeling was shared by some members of the American team, although it seemed the likes of Tiger Woods, David Duval and Phil Mickelson sided more with O'Meara. It was an amazing situation, but the gang of four soon moved the goalposts from wanting to be paid to play to requesting a donation to be made to a charity in their name. This was a whole different ball game, and essentially a way for them to squirm out of the controversy.

I do not know what came over them, because it was a farcical situation, albeit one I was more than happy to sit back and watch develop. Actually, I was loving it. I would never have said publicly that this was exactly the sort of situation we wanted, because it gives us a better chance under the 'united we stand, divided they fall' scenario, but there is no doubting that anything that stops the opposition gelling as a team and getting on together is good news for the other side. Ben knew this, and he was probably the best person to try to paper over the cracks.

It had all blown up again just before the start of the US PGA Championship, and this was a good move on Ben's part because it highlighted the fact that some of their players were being a bit dim to say the least. There was a noticeable split in their camp. Ben was not without support when he launched his attack, and I agreed with him entirely, as did a number of ex-Ryder Cup players, including Arnold Palmer. Ben knew he was right and thought it best to try to settle the issue a few weeks in advance. Had it rumbled on right into Ryder Cup week, the press would have loved it; without doubt it would have done the USA's chances a fair bit of harm. Our hope was that they were still knocking seven bells out of one another on the first morning's foursomes, but ultimately it probably did not make any difference. We certainly had a good chuckle over it though, not least on the bus back from the gala dinner to our hotel.

We were at the end of another extremely enjoyable day, and we were now getting very close to the reason we were there. Everybody seemed to be on top of everything, so there was no reason to lose any sleep (not that I ever do). I may have been a little biased, but I thought the atmosphere was wonderful. Everybody was still relaxed and happy.

The atmosphere at breakfast on the Thursday was little different to that of the previous two days, although I could sense things building to the extent that the players just wanted to get the last practice session out of the way so that they could get at the Americans.

Indeed, they did not want to practise at all, just to get the job started. Still with the exception of Olly, in his own estimation at least, they were playing well, and kick-off could not come quickly enough.

I ran through one or two things with the players and repeated what I had said at the beginning of the week: that I hoped to play everybody before the singles, but it was possible it would not happen that way, depending on how things went in each series. I would honestly not have believed you if you had told me before we set off that three players would not see action before the Sunday. That they had to sit out for the first two days was a reflection on how the starting eight performed, not on their own standard of play. It was an issue which everybody seemed to accept, though, and, despite a small amount of criticism from Jean Van de Velde afterwards, one which did not interfere with the overall spirit in the camp.

We were scheduled for a 9 a.m. to 9.30 a.m. tee-off, but I switched that to an hour later so the players could enjoy the gala dinner without having to worry about getting back to the hotel for an early start. They were all aware that there were only a few bits and bobs to be sorted out and really did not want another day's practice, although all were keen to play the crucial holes on the back nine. The only thing that absolutely had to be determined that morning was whether or not Olly's driver was behaving itself.

There was an official photo shoot once we arrived at the course, and we were pictured standing, sitting, crouching, kneeling, in the Lotus position, every which way. After that we were ready to go, but nobody had told the Americans, and some of their players were still waiting to tee off at the ninth at our time. A couple of their officials approached me, and I said, 'We changed our times and we'll be teeing off the ninth at ten o'clock.' There had obviously been a breakdown in communication somewhere along the line, and it seemed to throw them into disarray. Nobody more so than David Duval, who was still playing the eighth, and on his own, which struck me as being a bit odd. They seemed to be going out in any old fashion, but I could not work out whether or not it was a deliberate tactic. Whatever it was, confusion reigned.

We claimed our slots anyway, and Lee and Darren went out with Andrew and Jarmo, while Olly and Mechanico followed with Padraig and Jean. The second fourball was deliberate. I particularly wanted Olly and Padraig to be in the same group because I had told the former he would be replaced by the latter if he did not feel his driving was fit enough for the first morning's foursomes. Now was the right time, I felt, to let Olly see that if he was not quite right, Padraig was really ripping it. I had also spoken to Monty to ask if there was any pairing he would particularly like to have a go at; he said he had never played with Sergio, so I had no hesitation in fixing it. Monty also told me he wanted a leisurely lunch. There is nothing like a bunch of happy campers come Ryder Cup time.

And so to the question mark. I approached Olly on the fourteenth because the deadline for entering the starting foursomes line-up was approaching. His honesty was highly commendable. Although nearly there, he did not feel he was driving it well enough; it would be better, he said, to leave him out of that discipline in favour of Padraig. That settled it.

At various stages we discussed whether or not we should try to guess what the Americans might do and see if there was any advantage to be gained, but we could not come up with any suggestions worth following up. The only concession we decided to make in that direction was to put Monty and Paul out last on

Saturday afternoon, just in case the Americans were starting to second-guess us and maybe get an advantage themselves.

By the time we had finished Thursday practice, at 1 p.m., there was just time for a quick bite before the final press session, and then a rules meeting. The press spent most of their time with us looking for things which were not there. My answers may have disappointed them. No, I was not worried about the American pairings because if I started thinking too much about them it might be counter-productive. No, there was no hidden agenda behind Olly's withdrawal from the foursomes. No, I attached no significance to the fact that Sergio and Tiger Woods were in the same group, and no, none of Ben's pairings had surprised me. No, there was no deep thinking behind my own pairings, and no, I had not given Paul Lawrie to Monty to look after, rather Monty to Paul to look after (although I think everybody spotted that I might have been slightly exaggerating there).

But everybody there appeared to be in a happy mood and there was plenty of laughter, which was slightly bemusing because I was not trying to be funny. I could not understand why this bit of dialogue, for instance, should have brought the roof down. Question: Mark, can you tell me how Padraig learnt he was actually playing tomorrow? Answer: I said, 'Padraig, you're playing tomorrow with Miguel.' And for some unknown reason they laughed again when I was asked if I shared the rest of the golf world's excitement at the thought of Sergio and Tiger out there together. I had replied, 'Yes, I think it's extremely exciting.'

But there was one question which almost did my head in. This is exactly how it was asked: 'Mark, both Darren and Lee have made mention in recent weeks about Darren's head, the state of his head, and Lee saying he's probably the only player who could keep Darren's head on his shoulders. Do you agree with that? And what's the state of Darren's head right now, going into these matches?' Not even Julius Mason, their very efficient press officer, could resist adding to that: 'You asked for that one.' Fortunately, I was able to report that Darren's head had no ache.

If there had been plenty of laughter in the press room, the players were soon having a good chuckle at the rules meeting too. As usual, it started off quite sensibly as we discovered whether or not we were allowed to tread on our opponents' balls and poke them in the eye, then things degenerated into farce as we picked holes in everything John Paramor, from our tour, and Ed Hoard from America told us. Of the few serious issues raised, there was an unusual one from Dave McNeilly, Padraig's caddie. He asked if the caddies could go out before play started and roll balls on the greens in order to find out what putts were likely to do. I thought it quite clever of Dave to consider this, but thought it a touch iffy; John thought it might be best if we just spoke to the Americans and had a gentleman's agreement not to do it.

The meeting got so confusing that we had had enough by twenty to four, so we went to another briefing on what was going to happen, where we were going to sit and all the other things that matter during an opening ceremony. There were 400 yards to negotiate between clubhouse and podium without getting lost, falling over or wandering over to the putting green. We eventually lined up with the captains at the head of the procession and the rest following in alphabetical order. It seemed a long, long way as we followed the bagpipers, moving at snail's pace. It was like playing with Ken in the early 1980s – you never thought you were going to reach the green. It was a real relief to arrive at the podium. The atmosphere was nothing short of brilliant, and everybody was in a state of expectation and excitement because this was where it all kicked off. No more dinners or practice, just time to enter the fray.

The ceremony was well choreographed, although I was no less apprehensive about my speech, still thinking about Tuesday night when I had felt I might never put a sentence together again without assistance. I had learnt from that experience though: this time I wrote down some bullet points and did a better job, thank goodness. I avoided one booby trap, because on the list I had been given of players and their nations it stated that Paul Lawrie came from England, which for a Scot, I would assume, is one of the most severe forms of insult. I spotted it, but mentioned it nevertheless. Anything like that is quickly seized upon by the players and stored for use at a later date. The only thing I could remember about Ben's speech was something which only came back to me after the final day: 'We welcome you in the spirit of what Samuel Ryder started, and I hope that spirit never dies.'

There was a look bordering on relief among all the players after the opening ceremony, not just because I had got through a speech without making an idiot of myself, but because the long wait was just about over and we could concentrate totally on the reason we were there.

By this stage of the week the courtesy car drivers had realised we did not like being in a car for over an hour and were finding alternative routes, although that did not stop Monty's driver getting lost. 'How can they get lost? Haven't they been practising?' wondered Monty. 'He was from Connecticut, for heaven's sake.'

There was no set time for that night's team meeting, and in any case I did not have a lot to tell them because they all knew the starting line-up, but there were things to remind them about. One thing I deliberately did not tell them, although most, if not all, of them knew, was that Nick Faldo had sent a good luck letter. Similar missives from the likes of Seve and Ian Woosnam had been pinned on our noticeboard and were much appreciated. This one was not pinned up, because I took one look at it and could not believe Faldo had sent it. Not only had he had a serious barney with me relatively recently, but he had also slagged off Monty just before we came to Boston.

Faldo's attack on Monty fewer than two weeks before the Ryder Cup could not have come at a worse time, and was a follow-up to Monty's remark that he intended never to play in America full time. What that had to do with Faldo beats me, but it seemed he could not resist having a dig at one of his former partners. They may never have been close friends, but Monty had probably been a great admirer of the Englishman at one stage. It was a situation which no longer existed.

Perhaps Faldo did not like the fact that through Monty's performances and achievements and his own failings, the Scot was now in a position where he could look down rather than up at him, as he once had. Faldo said Monty liked 'fat cheques' and, by implication, accused the Scot of valuing money over major championships, including the Open. 'I don't know what he wants,' Faldo said of Montgomerie in the *Daily Mail*. 'I am surprised he has not done something different as a challenge, but he likes to earn his fat cheques each week. There is no harm in that if that's what motivates you. Most of us go for ten claret jugs.' Monty was also likened to Jumbo Ozaki, an unbelievable comparison considering the Japanese player's relatively modest standing in world golf: Ozaki has won a hundred times at home, but only once abroad, at the 1972 New

Zealand PGA Championship. 'It's a bit like that scenario,' Faldo was reported as saying. 'Great in his own backyard. He's comfortable, happy and knows he's only got to play half decent and he's going to be there. Even if he plays badly, he's the sort of guy who turns round a good score the next day and gets himself into contention. He goes out and wins a couple of hundred grand each week and goes home. I'd be comfortable if I did that every week.'

Faldo may have thought that with six major championships behind him he had a platform, but to launch that kind of diatribe against a fellow professional, friend and former team-mate was unforgivable, and Monty was entitled to feel upset. It was to his credit that he did not dignify Faldo's comments with a response. He may have many and varied opinions, but at least he knows when to air them and when to keep them to himself. It is a trick Faldo has still to master; show him a notebook or microphone these days and it seems he tends to spout off in similar mode to Tony Jacklin. To insult Monty the way Faldo did was stupid, and not one person in the team room had the slightest bit of sympathy with his sentiments. The outburst came at such a crucial time that I can only think it was directly designed to undermine the team's chances, and in the eyes of the whole team that was unpardonable.

Faldo's good luck letter was typed, and I think had his signature at the bottom. My first inclination was to throw it away, but first I decided to seek the views of a few other people, including some of the players, and everybody's reaction was the same: bin it. I had no hesitation accepting their advice. There was no room on our noticeboard for the words of somebody who we felt was obviously not 100 per cent behind us.

Not so the one from Seve Ballesteros, which served as a superb example of motivation for everybody. 'I can see the European team is full of energy and their minds are fresh,' he wrote. 'I am sure your experience will be able to get out all the best of their capacity. I will watch all the matches on television and send you all my encouragement and good vibrations. Undoubtedly victory is in your side.' There were similar sentiments from Ian Woosnam. 'Here's wishing you all the best,' he wrote. 'We're all rooting for you and know you can bring back the cup.' And comedian Jimmy Tarbuck touched all our funny bones when he wrote: 'I will be watching and wishing you all well. Beware of their wild card – it's Monica Lewinsky.'

It was a united force that listened to my final pre-match address. I told them that only the captain, not even the assistants, could give advice to any of the players, and Ken and Sam had to be careful in this respect. If they were out supporting a group they had to keep out of the way and say nothing. If they spotted or heard anything it had to be run through me. I spoke about how they would be nervous, and if team uniform trousers were brown on Friday then they would soon discover why.

The Ryder Cup is without doubt the most nerve-racking experience I have ever encountered. I can never forget playing with Howard Clark in 1989 against Curtis Strange and Payne Stewart at a time when the former had just won the US Open and the latter the US PGA. It was the Saturday afternoon. A win, and Europe would have gone into the last day two points ahead; a loss, and it would have been all square. There was a helluva lot resting on the outcome of this match, and both pairs were beginning to feel it. We were one down playing the sixteenth when Howard hit in to twelve feet, while I was thirty feet away and both Americans the same. One of them got up to putt, and he was just about to hit it when he backed away, unsure as to whether it was their turn or ours. Referee John Paramor was called in and, after pacing it out, decided it was me to go, which I promptly did. I promptly missed. Curtis then lined up his putt, looked from both sides, back and front, consulted Payne, and took immense care and six practice swings before backing away, saying to his team-mate, 'I think it's best if you go.' So Payne got up. He had a similar line, consulted his partner, and missed.

Because both Howard and I are from Yorkshire there was a huge following from the county, and it was obvious they were getting slightly bored with the time it was taking. We had been on the green for ten minutes and only two people had putted, and now it was Curtis' turn again. He looked from both sides and ends, took six practice putts, and was just about to hit it when the doubts hit him again. He stepped away and called Payne over. They had another conflab, and by the time Curtis was ready again there was a deathly silence because people were falling asleep. Curtis had another look and took another six practice putts before hitting a putt which came up just short. Just as it stopped rolling a voice from the crowd shouted out, 'Tha shouldn't 'ave rushed it, Curtis!'

It was a supreme example of how the occasion can affect your nervous system, although it took me a few holes to realise what Costantino Rocca was going through four years later when we were paired together against Corey Pavin and Jim Gallacher Jr. It was Costa's first game in the Ryder Cup and I could see he was a bit edgy, so I tried to chat to him. Whatever I said the response was always the same: nothing. The Americans were on a hot streak, and I thought Costa was just settling in, but when we went two down after two holes I thought it strange that he had not said one word. I told him the match was far from over and did all I could to make him feel at ease, but still there was not a sound. To try to involve him more and at least get a word out of him, I asked him for the line on the next green; he simply walked over, took a look and pointed with his putter. It was only then that I realised he was just too nervous to speak.

The Americans were virtually unstoppable, and when Pavin holed his second shot on the fifth we were four down, struggling badly, and Costa still had not spoken, although I felt sure he must be getting over his nerves. Through the trees came light, and it looked like we might win the next when Gallacher went in the lake and Pavin finished in trees. We were in a good position. Costa hit in to 25 feet, and when I asked him what the club should be he just pointed to my four iron. It looked as if Pavin had no shot, but he pulled out a two iron and hit a low cut which pitched on the bank of the lake on the left, skittered along the edge of the water, fell off the bank, came up on to the top and rolled on to the green two feet from the pin. Rocca looked at me and opened his mouth for the first time. 'Shit! Shit! Shit,' he said. Costa got over his nerves and was a cornerstone of our victories in 1995 and 1997.

Nerves manifest themselves in all kinds of ways, and I wanted to ensure all the players, particularly the first-timers, were aware what might happen and not to think they were the only ones being affected. The first tee is always a tester, particularly in foursomes, because if you make a mess there is nobody to cover. It is the hardest shot of the week, unless you are coming down eighteen with everything resting on it. I wanted them all to understand the importance of not playing a shot until they were absolutely ready. If they were not prepared or unhappy about anything, then they were just to step away and take their time. When you are nervous there is always an inclination to rush a shot, and that can be fatal. With a relatively inexperienced side, any move in that direction could easily become magnified. If they had any reservations about playing too slowly, then I assured them that unless they gave us set times, as in normal tournaments, nobody would be penalised. If anybody was done for slow play in a Ryder Cup it would signal the equivalent of World War Three. Battleships would be heading for Boston from British waters.

I felt this advice readily sank in, but I reiterated the importance of focus all the same, and hammered home my mantra: 'If you have two putts for the hole, then take them.' It was greeted, as I expected, by a chorus of derision.

The guys not directly involved were advised to play a few holes behind the matches, but they had to keep a two-hole gap behind the last match. If they were supporting a match, they were to walk inside the ropes and not climb on buggies too much. They had also to be careful of practice-putting after holes had been completed, although if they thought their opponents were doing it to try to disrupt their rhythm then they were to do exactly the same, wait for them to finish and then move on together.

I ended my little address by telling them that we were playing well, we were not over-confident but ready to perform, and if we did not win then we would give them a helluva fright. Unfortunately, that was exactly the way it turned out.

It was a relaxed meeting with plenty of laughter. They appeared to be in exactly the right frame of mind, although there was one slight doubt when I strolled into the video room and found Darren on his own. When a player wanders off then you have to wonder if something has happened, but he was 100 per cent OK and had just disappeared to find a quiet place where he could enjoy a four-foot cigar. Mentally, Darren had been tremendously positive all week and he was very strong and settled. That was good news.

We were all relaxing and slouching around when HRH Prince Andrew, the Duke of York, came in to wish us luck, and we invited him to stay for a while to watch the team video compiled by Jeff Harvey of Tour Productions which showed short clips of each player accompanied by a very emotive background of music. We had had one at Oak Hill in 1995, and it was extremely good, not particularly for motivational purposes but to have a laugh at and for the purpose of putting people in the right frame of mind, watching themselves holing good putts and acknowledging the crowd. Lee Westwood attracted the loudest laughter as pictures of him wearing local garb at the Malaysian Open came up, and there were others of Mechanico sipping champagne and Darren in a fast car, and even a clip of me holing a bunker shot – something of a collector's item.

We all watched in amusement, along with Prince Andrew. As soon as it finished Sam jumped up to switch it off, and the television reverted to the channel it was on before the video was put in. For some unknown reason, unless Sergio had been messing about with the knobs, it was on the Playboy Channel, and Sam immediately said, 'I'm sorry, you're not supposed to watch this kind of thing, sir.' Prince Andrew nodded and turned away in a very royal manner.

Sometimes the atmosphere can be a little muted if there is a royal around, simply because everybody's language is careful, but Prince Andrew is brilliant and balances it very well, considering it must be difficult for him to know where to pitch.

The show over, it was time for the wives to mop their husbands' brows, fluff up their pillows and tuck them in, leaving Sam, Ken and I with the girls to have a nightcap. As I said, I had imposed no drinks ban or time curfew, but nobody had had to be sent to bed because you can get away with that sort of thing less and less these days, in every sport. People have tried to burn the candle at both ends in the past, but the modern level of competition is such that you just cannot afford to do it. Everything is too intense to mess about, and even though golfers have a longer career than most sportsmen and women, you want to make the most of it. One bad spell these days and you can lose your card and playing rights very quickly. The competition and incentives are such that you have to keep as fit and healthy as you can, and be bright-eyed and bushy-tailed.

As we sat there with a glass of Chardonnay, looking back over the week, we were a happy bunch. I had been swotting for a year, and the first part of the examination was over. I felt I had not missed anything, and between the six of us I thought the plan to cover all bases had been achieved. We had done just about all we could, and now it was a question of reacting to how the pairings played.

Everybody in Team Europe was ready. We raised our glasses for a goodnight toast: Let the games begin.

8 Six Appeal

THE DAY FINALLY DAWNED, and we were all in our courtesy cars by 6.30 a.m. in readiness for breakfast at the course. I shared a ride with Ken and Sam so that we could go over everything and check there was nothing we had forgotten. Attention to detail had been our hallmark, and there was no reason to change now. We had had a lot of brains working on the preparation and if we had got it wrong then we all deserved to be strung up. Things seemed to be in place, although there was the daily problem of the drivers getting lost or going to the wrong gate and having to turn round and try again.

Even though it was barely light, there were people everywhere, queueing in their hundreds for the gates to open at 7 a.m. so they could watch the players practise. I was more relaxed than I would have been had I been playing. When you play, you prepare as well as you can and do all your homework, but when you get out on the course, even if you have done all the swotting and revision, you can fail the examination hopelessly. It is much the same for the captain, but I felt I was starting in the right way, even though I would not hit a shot. I knew I could be held responsible at any stage, and that was something I was perfectly prepared for, otherwise I would not have taken the job in the first place. I was both excited and looking forward to it, but, above all, I was hoping like hell that we would get off smoothly, and at least keep up. 'A solid start, please' was all I asked. There is always the threat, playing away from home, that if you start slowly it can turn into a quick result – against you.

We eventually found the right gate and our car finally pulled up in front of the building where the locker rooms were situated. Even though the gates had not yet been opened to the public there were still plenty of people shouting out encouragement and wishing us luck. It was much appreciated. A route had been devised in the building which ensured we did not go anywhere near the Americans, to ensure there was no invasion of privacy.

I was a bit edgy, so I did not have much breakfast, just fruit, scrambled eggs, bacon, toast, croissants, a blueberry muffin and half a dozen chocolate chip cookies. There is nothing like a sportsman's snack to start the day. The guys were a little bit quieter than normal, but it was nothing to be worried about, and the Golf Channel was forever on television so we had something to laugh at, although they did a great job all week and were very nice about us. The mood was good, and I did not say much because anything that needed to be said had already been said. The boys were munching away contentedly; I was there just in case anybody needed to speak to me or they wanted something. Nothing we could do now would alter things.

Sergio was his normal self, extremely chirpy and without a care in the world. Still only nineteen, he had slipped into the team as if he had been there for the last five years. Monty was very relaxed too, which had become the norm for him, although as the weekend progressed circumstances would change his mood, if not his ability to play golf of the highest calibre under the most trying of circumstances. Jesper had not called for any volcanic dust, and Lee seemed to be coping admirably with Nottingham Forest's poor start to the season. If they needed anything, they did not ask for it. All they wanted was to get out there on to a course which Ben had set up, quite rightly, with his own team in mind.

I wandered over to the putting green at 7.45 a.m. just to be there, so that the players knew I was knocking around in case they needed a banana or waterproofs out of their lockers. I checked my walkie-talkie, making sure of a direct link to Ken and Sam, among others, although it was not a crowded network, just the people I might need to get hold of in a hurry. We used the system to update information, and for general chit-chat about what each group was doing, although during the match we also used miniature radios tuned in to BBC Radio's Five Live to keep us in touch with events all over the course. I would hear a cheer here or there and wonder what it signified. I am not very good at decoding cheers, probably because I get so few when I am playing. It can be a question of second-guessing, and there is nothing worse than thinking you have just won a hole only to find you have lost two.

I saw Ben on the first tee, and we shook hands and wished each other luck. We were both glad kick-off was imminent because it had been a long year from being made captain to getting to this point. In Ben's case it had been two years, and he had probably had to do a lot more organisation at the course than I had, although he played a bit less than I did. The only other American I had any real contact with at that stage was a very touching moment with Payne Stewart. He went over to this little old lady who was behind a barrier and gave her a big hug and kiss before walking away. I gave him a little smile, and he said, 'You've got to look after your mum, haven't you?' to which I replied, 'You're absolutely right.'

It was time for the morning foursomes to go, with Monty and Paul facing David Duval and Phil Mickelson. Monty had cleverly conned Paul into taking the first tee shot, which was without doubt the hardest of the week, but one he felt his fellow Scot was more than capable of handling. It had been mentioned by Paul as a source of amusement that a guy who had won the money list seven times in a row had forced the opening shot on somebody who was playing in the Ryder Cup for the first time. Come the moment, Paul seemed ready to deal with the task, as he had with everything he had had to deal with since winning the Open. It was a good job, because just before they teed off Monty had been in fits of laughter at something the referee had said, and probably would not have been in any condition to take it anyway.

Paul spanked the first tee shot away, and we were off and running. The 33rd Ryder Cup was heading towards one of the most epic duels of all time. Nobody could have guessed then that it was also on its way towards its most controversial conclusion.

I saw every group off, and I wished all the Americans good luck, because I was looking forward to a good contest with some high-class golf. I would not have liked it to be a whitewash either way, although it was unlikely to be in our favour on their soil. I thought we had a chance of winning, but felt the odds were against us because of where we were, and the fact that they had a strong team. A lot depended on the run of the ball, and we got it for the first two days, although not by a massive margin. The Americans more than made up for it on the last day.

When they set off, USA were the favourites, although I knew there was plenty of bite in the 'underpuppies'. I knew intimately how good some of our players were, the Americans did not. To say I was a proud captain was an understatement.

Sergio immediately looked a Ryder Cup veteran, and I felt confident his partnership with Jesper would yield points. I could have won a lot of money from the Americans on this belief, because facing my second pairing was no less a figure than world number one Tiger Woods, with former Open champion Tom Lehman. They looked a very strong duo.

With Olly sitting out, the third pairing of Mechanico and Padraig was the only all-rookie pairing, but as with all the others, I had no worries that they would not be up to the task of facing Davis Love III and Payne Stewart. I had similar confidence in Lee and Darren, who were really looking forward to being off last, and in a position where the result of the morning series would hinge on what they were doing. Darren was really up for it because he had been good in practice, and once he gets on a roll there is no telling how well he can play.

If I had any concerns, they were about whether or not they had taken everything they needed with them. In practice they were always forgetting things, and we had to arrange a supply line linked to the clubhouse to ship out waterproofs, power bars, chocolate and drinks, while Monty was forever ordering 'tuna sandwiches with absolutely no chunks'. Jarmo was invariably ready for a hefty snack just an hour after devouring his cereal and chicken pasta mountain. I thought getting things out there on match day would prove difficult because of the crowds, but – wonders never cease – they got everything they wanted. Now all they needed was a little luck to go along with their undoubted ability.

Where to go and what to do was not as straightforward as it might appear, once all four pairings were out on the course. As captain, you want desperately to make yourself useful while at the same time not being exactly sure how to go about it. I guessed I should just try to be around if there was a crucial match, and come up the last two holes to offer whatever support or guidance was required. I also figured I could be useful in terms of handing back information from the par threes to the following groups, telling them what clubs had been used by the players ahead. If it made the difference between a par and a birdie all week then the exercise would be deemed a success: Ryder Cups these days are often decided by a shot here or there. Had there been four short holes it would have been virtually impossible, but the three were nicely spaced out. Relaying the news would not be a problem for the first two days at least, although things were likely to be more complicated during the singles. I did have Ken and Sam to help, but they could observe only and had to report back to me. They are experts, however, and the feedback from them was of the highest order.

Some players find information important, others do not. Jesper, for instance, was not worried about knowing what anybody else hit because he had total confidence in his own clubbing, and was not certain how hard other players might be hitting the ball in any case. But if Sergio wanted help, then I made sure his caddie, Jerry Higginbotham, had all the right data. If the wind was right to left and a player had hit a soft fade, I would watch how the ball reacted and report back to the following groups.

As the groups progressed on the first morning there was absolutely no hint of the crowd trouble which would spoil the final day. Our public relations exercise seemed to be paying off; if anything, it was the Americans who came in for a little bit of stick. When David Duval came on the first tee, somebody shouted out, 'Hey, David, play your ranking.' That was bordering on abuse and unpleasant, and was probably a by-product of the pay-for-play issue and other com-

I've been fortunate enough to play in seven Ryder Cup matches. Here I'm putting on the seventh green at The Belfry in 1993 (Photo: Action Images)

The team sweaters worn by the European wives and girlfriends at The Belfry in 1993 were something my wife, Jane, and I wanted to move away from at Brookline. In the centre is Suzanne Torrance, wife of Sam, and the lady captain for The Belfry in 2001 (Photo: private collection)

José Maria Olazábal and Payne Stewart enjoy each other's company at The Belfry, 1993 (Photo: private collection)

Above Darren Clarke,
Sergio Garcia and Sam
Torrance compare notes
(Photo; private collection)

Right Spanish 'Boy
Wonder' Sergio Garcia
and Jane. She assures
me this was merely an
example of team spirit
(Photo: private collection)

Top left A team to be proud of (Photo: Stuart Franklin/Action Images)

Bottom left My two right-hand men: Sam Torrance and Ken Brown. Their assistance was invaluable (Photo: Stuart Franklin/Action Images)

Right Darren Clarke relaxes during practice in his own inimitable style (Photo: Stuart Franklin/Action Images)

Below You can take a horse to water . . .! Jane supplies me with some liquid refreshment during a press conference (Photo: private collection)

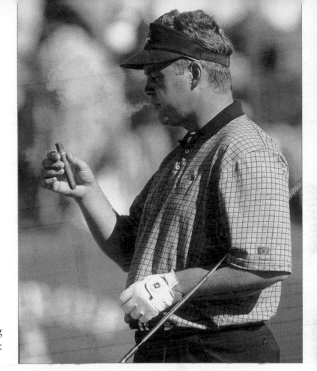

Above Jesper Parnevik and Sergio Garcia struck up a wonderful partnership
(Photo: Stuart Franklin/Action Images)

Left The Knights of the Round Table convene in the team room (Photo: private collection)

Right Justin Leonard has just holed his monster birdie putt on the seventeenth green. (Photo: Rusty Jarrett/ Allsport)

Below Rather belatedly, attempts are made to clear the green. Someone has just remembered that José Maria Olazábal still has a putt to take the contest to the eighteenth (Photo: Andrew Redington/Allsport)

Left Payne Stewart attempts to calm down the crowd during his singles match with Monty. He was fighting a losing battle (Photo: Stuart Franklin/Action Images)

Below At times, spectators' behaviour crossed the line between enthusiasm and unacceptable rowdiness. I was witness to scenes that I never wish to see repeated on a golf course (Photo: Stephen Munday/Allsport)

ments about the Ryder Cup being just an exhibition match. The taunts would become even more distasteful as the Americans struggled for points early on. 'What kind of exhibition is this?' and 'How much you being paid to play like this?' were among the more vitriolic.

I found it strange, because David had never really said boo to a goose in his life as far as I was aware. I had had a chat with him at the US PGA the previous month and he told me how, after he had become world number one for a time earlier in the year, people suddenly seemed to think he was a world authority on everything from golf to nuclear physics, breaststroke to breast implants. He thought it ridiculous that people should assume that just because he was good at what he did, it made him the same in every field. I have always believed he has conducted himself extremely well, although, along with several other Americans, he appeared to go a bit loopy on the final day. However, for people to shout out what they did was incredibly rude.

I was hoping that all the Americans, players and spectators alike, were in for a rude awakening. The early signs were encouraging. As soon as we nipped ahead in a couple of matches I was confident we would go into lunch with a lead, which made my job much easier. The morning-session boys were not just playing solidly, but extremely well. And it was not that the Americans were playing badly. Keeping three pairs the same and just bringing in Olly alongside Mechanico seemed the right decision; it would have been a mistake to alter things too much at that stage. I am sure the three who did not get a game would all have been capable of good golf, but they were up against proven form.

If filling in the pairings had been easy, telling the players who would be left without a game on the first day was not. I felt it important that I should speak to them first, and I did. It was not a nice experience, for me or for them, but it came with the job and had to be done. Better that they hear it from me than from the grapevine. Jean was particularly disappointed, but he took it well. I am sure Andrew and Jarmo felt exactly the same, but never once while the matches were in progress did any of them give me or anybody else any reason to doubt their commitment to the team cause. They were all very supportive, and showed not the slightest dissent. Jean has subsequently said that everybody in the team should play before the singles. I respect his point of view, but I do not agree with it.

It can be a quick turnaround between morning and afternoon matches. Once you have finished the first you are automatically given a minimum twenty minutes before starting the second, which allows just about enough time to grab a snack, change your underwear or, in Sergio's case, run round the clubhouse leaping into the air. The mood was nothing short of fantastic at lunch – an atmosphere which would be retained all the way through until the last day. We were on their territory, and we had the start we wanted. We could not have asked for more. We were not just ahead at the break, but playing well, which makes a huge difference. We felt so good that we were totally unconcerned as to who the Americans put out in their revised pairings, but if they thought I would change my order, they were wrong.

Ben had called for a new deck, and it looked like he had been shuffling it all morning. With the exception of Sutton and Maggert, the only Americans to earn a point that morning, the rest were all new partnerships. Love, with Stewart in the morning, now had Leonard alongside, while Mickelson, a loser alongside Duval, had Furyk as a tee-time guest; Duval would team up with

Woods for the first time and, as it turned out, the last. The numbers one and two in the world would end the day as they started it, pointless, which just goes to show how unpredictable matchplay can be.

Our afternoon fortunes would turn out very similar to the morning, only better. Things started out fairly even, then ever so gradually we started to take control. It was a wonderful feeling to see a preponderance of European colours on the leaderboards, and at one stage it looked like we were heading for a clean sweep, but we had to settle for dropping half a point out of the four available.

Day 1 Morning Foursomes

Match 1: Colin Montgomerie/Paul Lawrie v. David Duval/Phil Mickelson

Not many rookies would enjoy taking the first shot of the 33rd Ryder Cup, and I can think of quite a few experienced campaigners who would feel the same way, but Paul Lawrie was completely unfazed. Paul let neither himself nor the team down on that first tee.

This was a very strong pairing, one which I hoped could give us not just an early edge, but also an example the rest could follow. They did not disappoint me or the rest of the lads, although it was quite a long time before they established a superiority over their rivals. However, once they had them in their grip, it was vice-like.

Duval and Mickelson ended a five-hole deadlock with the first birdie of the match on the sixth hole, despite the former driving into the crowd. A lucky bounce had allowed the ball to come to rest in short rough, where the latter showed off one of the strongest parts of his repertoire with a flop shot to two feet.

American cheers died down when the match was squared with a par on the next hole, and there was almost silence when a second successive birdie produced another win on the eighth, Paul hitting his approach to five feet and Monty doing the rest.

European joy was short-lived too, and the match entered the back nine all square, but it was not long before we started taking command. Paul looked as if he had been to the Ryder Cup born, and was by no means the junior partner as the first match headed for home. The tenth was the fourth successive hole to change hands and came courtesy of an American bogey from a three-putt. It was the second time we had gone ahead, and Duval and Mickelson could not pull back.

They fell further behind on the twelfth when Paul rolled the ball in from eight feet for a hole-winning par. The Americans were in terminal decline, and went three adrift after hole fourteen when Mickelson missed for a half from six feet. Two more halves, and the match was over. Our first point was on the board – only another thirteen needed to retain the trophy.

'It was fantastic,' Paul admitted afterwards. 'The experience of hitting the first tee shot was not a particularly nice one, but I'll be able to look back on it now, especially now that my heart's back to a normal beat.' A gracious Mickelson paid tribute to my boys when he said, 'For them to play foursomes on a US Open course without making bogey is very impressive.'

Europe win 3 & 2

Match 2: Jesper Parnevik/Sergio Garcia v. Tiger Woods/Tom Lehman

The Americans definitely fancied getting something out of this match, but not as much as we did. Sergio does not appear to know the meaning of the word 'pressure', and alongside the experienced Jesper Parnevik I was convinced we had a pairing capable of producing points every time they teed up. They let nobody down, and were a credit to everybody, including themselves.

But they had to do it the hard way against the world number one and the former Open champion. There was no disgrace in losing the first hole to Lehman's thirty-foot chip-in for birdie, the Americans already chalking up this match as a win when their side went further ahead shortly afterwards, Lehman's chip over a bunker converted by Woods.

Two holes later, we were back level: an American bogey on the sixth gifted us one, then Jesper rolled in a birdie putt on the seventh. They would never again go behind, eventually taking the lead on the twelfth as Lehman and Woods proved they were not quite the dream pairing their supporters expected by three-putting, although it was from more than forty feet.

For somebody who has so much energy and enthusiasm, Sergio has no problem concentrating, and it was obvious in his demeanour that he wanted his first Ryder Cup match win at the first attempt, especially when one of his opponents was the best player in the world. Whatever the Americans produced, Jesper and Sergio matched, and after four successive halves, the match ended on the seventeenth when the Swede delivered a decisive birdie. No matter what happened elsewhere, we would go into lunch no worse than all square, but we were hungry for more.

Europe win 2 & 1

Match 3: Miguel Angel Jiménez/Padraig Harrington v. Davis Love III/Payne Stewart

José Maria Olazábal stood down to concentrate on getting his driving on track for the afternoon fourballs, and Ireland's Padraig Harrington stepped in for his debut. Like Sergio Garcia and Paul Lawrie before him, he looked as if he had been a part of the Ryder Cup for years. So did Miguel.

Padraig had impressed in practice as much as anybody, and he carried his form into the match, although he was powerless to prevent the Americans from taking an early initiative. But this match would turn out to be as close as any there had been before.

Birdies on the third and fourth won both for the home pair, and we could not afford to slip further behind. The USA had every chance to take a hammer to our hopes on the fifth, but three-putted. We grew in strength from that moment on, even though we could not benefit on the fifth because we also needed three to get down. Love and Stewart would regret their lapse because they were pulled back on the sixth with our first sub-par return, a tap-in from Padraig after Miguel's wonderful bunker shot. Our second birdie, on the tenth, pulled the match back to all square, and two holes later we took the lead for the first time, a par good enough on the twelfth to bring success.

A regulation figure was also good enough to see the Americans draw level on the seventeenth, so we had now the prospect of the first match to head down the eighteenth, a hole that can be as intimidating as the first. Love and Stewart had been there several times before, but their greater experience would not be decisive. Padraig and Miguel could be immensely proud of their debut and the half point that came with it.

Match halved

Match 4: Lee Westwood/Darren Clarke v. Hal Sutton/Jeff Maggert

Nobody was looking forward to the matches more than the Englishman and the Ulsterman, both of whom had made their debuts in the previous encounter in Spain. They wanted to play together and I had been perfectly happy to grant their wish, confident they would make a very strong pairing. And so they proved, although, despite high-quality golf, it did not work out for them in this match.

It was a tribute to the standard of play from both teams that apart from the opening hole, when an American bogey gave us an early advantage, every other win by either side was achieved with a birdie. Our first, on the fourth, took us two up, and for quite some time we looked capable of hitting the halfway mark of the first day without having lost one match. Sutton had been having a very good season though, and Maggert had proved what a wily match player he was by winning the first ever World Golf Championship event earlier in the season in California.

They hit back with a trio of successive birdies, starting on the sixth, and headed home one up. Lee and Darren dug in and stayed with the Americans, but when they failed to birdie the par five fourteenth they slipped to two down, and the match ended with another American birdie on the sixteenth.

'You can't do much against six birdies and the rest pars after they'd bogeyed the first,' Lee said. Neither was particularly downhearted, although they were disappointed. They had lost playing well rather than badly, and felt that their time would come.

USA win 3 & 2

Afternoon Fourballs

Match 5: Colin Montgomerie/Paul Lawrie v. Davis Love III/Justin Leonard

The Scots were happy to play the lead role again in the afternoon, and I got the impression they would be happy to take on all-comers. It was a new pairing of Love and Leonard selected to face them, and the duel turned into an epic, one of the best matches of the entire competition.

Although the galleries could not resist trying to unsettle Monty, their efforts were counter-productive. The more jibes hurled at him, the greater his resolve to silence them through the sheer weight of his game. It became obvious very early on that he would not be beaten inside or outside the ropes.

The first eight holes were halved, but Leonard finally invited American cheers with a birdie on the par five ninth, eventually cancelled by a Monty three on the par four thirteenth. Paul followed it with an eagle on the next, but it was not good enough to win the hole, Love following him in for what would prove a very crucial half. Two more halved holes followed, which meant that whatever happened on the seventeenth, the match would go all the way to the wire.

A Monty birdie on seventeen at least took one possibility out of the equation: only America could lose now, our worst result a half. It looked as if we would just sneak it, but Love holed a long putt he was 10–1 on to miss on the final green, and honours were even.

Paul admitted afterwards that the result was a fair one. 'They were two tough matches and very tiring,' he said.

Match halved

Match 6: Jesper Parnevik/Sergio Garcia v. Phil Mickelson/Jim Furyk

If the top match featured a significant number of halved holes, this one contained very few. But it did have plenty of birdies and excitement, and featured the continued emergence of Sergio Garcia as a world force.

Jesper needed no introduction at this level, and his play, particularly over the first ten holes, was of the highest standard, amazing not only his partner and opponents, but also himself. He made five birdies and an eagle in that stretch, yet we were still only two holes up, and that lead disappeared in the next two. It was somewhat predictable that although Jesper had done all the serious damage, it would be Sergio who would step forward, or run in his case, to claim the glory.

The Americans were blowing against a hurricane, because although they shot a ten-under-par 62 between them, they were still turned over. Jesper went to the turn in 29, four shots better than the Americans' combined best balls. After the first six holes had been birdied by one side or the other, Jesper produced a candidate for shot of the week with his nine-iron approach to the 378-yard eighth. The applause when it fell into the hole was led by Prince Andrew; Sergio showed what he thought about it by charging down the fairway and hoisting his partner in the air. Jesper was far from finished, and soon afterwards was launching another spectacular shot towards the hole. Hitting out of thick rough on the tenth he hit a high draw to just six feet from the hole. It was not conceded, but on this day it was a definite gimme, and Jesper duly finished it off.

As Jesper's show came towards a grand finale, Sergio entered the action with a marvellous chip-in on the par five fourteenth for eagle. It was to Mickelson and

Furyk's credit that they took the pair all the way. Rarely, if ever, will they shoot so low again and lose.

Sergio, still an amateur six months before the match, paid tribute to his partner afterwards. 'It was a fantastic day, and two points for Europe is the most important thing, not two points for me. Jesper was unbelievable. The first ten holes he played were among the best I have ever seen and definitely it was the most enjoyable day's golf I've ever experienced.' Jesper reciprocated. 'When I needed Sergio over the last five or six holes he was right there,' he said.

Europe win 1 up

Match 7: José Maria Olazábal/Miguel Angel Jiménez v. Hal Sutton/Jeff Maggert

Olly had typified the spirit in the camp by sacrificing himself for the morning session, appreciating the first rule of foursomes play: the necessity to hit the ball straight as often as possible (that ingredient, although extremely useful, is not as important in fourball because of the cover available from your partner). But Olly's Ryder Cup record says everything about his commitment to Europe's cause, and he was anxious to get involved in the fourballs, replacing Padraig Harrington, my only change from the morning line-up.

From the moment Miguel birdied the opening hole, we would never lose the lead against what had been America's strongest partnership in the morning session. Maggert was not as impressive as he had been, and had to rely on Sutton to keep the USA in the match, but it was too big a job to do on his own. Mechanico increased our lead to two holes after four, and although America claimed the eleventh, they immediately surrendered the twelfth, and a succession of halves meant another success for us.

Sutton was generous in his appreciation of my pair afterwards. 'The key to getting on top of somebody in matchplay is to do things ahead of them, not on top of them,' he said. 'Today we were always having to follow them in. Any time you play Spaniards, they are always very good,' he added. 'They all play the same game: a great game.'

Europe win 2 & 1

Match 8: Lee Westwood/Darren Clarke v. David Duval/Tiger Woods

I had no hesitation keeping the two friends together, while the USA were no doubt licking their lips in anticipation of a feast to come, as Ben Crenshaw put the world's top two players together. Lee and Darren could not believe their luck: there was nothing more likely to tickle their taste buds than a match against the best in the world. Tiger had his pal Michael Jordan cheering him on, and ex-president George Bush took a very close interest in the match, but it is doubtful my pair saw them because they were so intent on winning after losing their opener in the morning. Although with different partners, neither Woods nor Duval had troubled the scorer in the morning either, so something was bound to give here.

Such was the standard and competitiveness of this match that there was never more than one hole in it at any stage, but that was almost predictable, considering all four are ranked in the world's top twenty. We twice gave back an early initiative, and a Woods chip-in birdie at the tenth meant the USA had the lead for the first time in the match. Woods pumped a fist and high-fived Duval; all my boys did was roll up their sleeves and take up the challenge.

Darren immediately nullified the advantage with a birdie, and Lee cancelled out Woods' birdie on the next. Another match was destined to go all the way when the two pairs reached the seventeenth tee all square, but by the time they left the green, Darren had birdied, and again we could not lose. Unlike Love and Leonard earlier, however, Woods and Duval could not rescue a half. Europe had taken three and a half out of four in the afternoon.

'We holed a few, they missed a few, but we made the putts at the right time,' said Darren.

It had been an outstanding day's golf. We had enjoyed more of the roll of the ball, but not by that much, because the USA had made no small contribution to this exhibition of how to play the game at the highest level.

Europe win 1 up

USA 2 EUROPE 6

Although I may have been stating the obvious to the world's press when I said it had been a good day for us, I was particularly eager to impress on them that it was just one day out of three, and that there would be no complacency in the camp. Winning six points was a bonus, but the rookies had done no more or less than I expected, even if they did seem to have surprised the assembled scribes. There was a lot of interest in Sergio, but I was quick to emphasise the importance of his partner Jesper, the perfect foil. 'Jesper knows exactly how to play with Sergio, when to let him loose and when to reign him in,' I said. 'All I do with Sergio is feed him chocolate and watch him go.'

I could not go along with the theory that we had inflicted psychological damage on the Americans, particularly Tiger Woods and David Duval, who had ended the day without so much as half a point between them. Anybody can lose a couple of matches, even the top two in the world rankings, but that did not make them lesser players and they were unlikely to be mentally impaired by their experiences. Their powers of recovery and of playing good golf would not be underestimated.

Tough questions followed. 'What do you figure was the best decision you made today as captain?' I replied, 'I had a hamburger for lunch instead of a turkey sandwich, and I really enjoyed it,' and added, 'I also took a lot of chocolate out for the boys, and they like that, because they do snack well.' I could not understand why everybody was laughing. I was being perfectly serious. Really, too much is made of the captain's influence.

I was asked what went into the decisions about pairings, and I said that it helped that none of their nations was at war with one another. Which was harder: playing, or being captain? That was an easy one, because watching is a lot easier than playing. 'I can get to a toilet whenever I want and not bother about missing shots,' I said. 'I can also nip back for a sandwich and do whatever I want, plus my knees aren't shaking when there's a six-foot putt to be holed. I can be a pretty iffy player at times.' Somebody wondered if a part of me wished to be out there playing, and I was honest when I said that having seen the boys practise for three days and then through one match day I would not have added anything to the team. They did not need somebody like me missing it from four feet. There had been quite a few putts like that, and it was much less nerve-racking watching them being holed or missed than having to do it myself.

We had been granted a few breaks, and several putts were dropped at crucial times, but I was far too much of a realist to believe anything other than it might be role reversal time the following day, such is the volatility of this form of golf. We had come out on top 6–2, but I would not dream of saying we were the superior side. Our only plan was to try to get as many points as possible before we entered Sunday's singles. 'You get peaks and troughs in every Ryder Cup, and today we had a peak,' I noted. 'We had the luck go our way, and there's every chance that at some stage here it will not go our way.'

I was also asked if I had given my players any advice, or interfered at all, so I explained that my duty was to hand out chocolate bars and tuna sandwiches without chunks if requested, and to be on hand if anybody fancied having a moan, although nobody had that day. And I liked to be there if somebody was unsure about tactics. 'We had a very bad ten to fifteen minutes this afternoon where we lost a few holes, and I tried to be in the right place then,' I said. 'I'm there for the players, although I might not be much use, but

I made absolutely certain that I wasn't sticking my nose in where it wasn't wanted.'

If some of my answers were considered slightly offbeat, I made sure everybody knew where I was coming from when it was suggested my players had deliberately played slowly. 'Absolutely not,' I said. 'I don't think Ben or myself would ever stoop to any sort of gamesmanship. It would never even enter my head to do anything remotely underhand.'

Back in the team room were a lot of chuffed players – an expression which has not travelled across the pond. Nobody would have guessed at the start of play that we would drop just half a point of the four on offer in the afternoon, but that is precisely what happened. I got most of the guys together at the course before I had to put in the following day's pairings and told them that the way things had turned out, I did not think I had a choice but to stick with the guys who had given us a 6–2 lead, at least for the Saturday morning session, and everybody, without exception, agreed.

Everyone had a smile on their face, with the possible exception of Monty. It was not only understandable, but also an early indication of how things would develop over the weekend for the rock of our team. It was starting to turn nasty behind the ropes. There was plenty of name-calling coming from the galleries, and Monty had attracted the nickname of Tuna because of a similarity in appearance to American football coach Bill Parcells. There were other similarities: both were extremely good at what they did, and both liked to voice their opinions. But it quickly became apparent that the crowd were not doing it in praise of his good looks and magnificent golf game. It was definitely not used as a term of endearment. Monty was absolutely livid at the abuse he was receiving. He was as cross as I have ever seen him, and he walked off the course extremely briskly. He left the clubhouse just as quickly, before he was tempted to rearrange it.

Unlike certain players on tour who have been known to inflict severe damage on furniture, their own clubs and occasionally caddies, Monty is not a locker-room wrecker. The legendary Danny Goodman once broke his caddie's ankle when lashing out at a European Tour event after hitting a bad shot. He intended to bury his club in the ground, but succeeded only in embedding it in his caddie's lower leg. Monty resisted the temptation to seek retribution on an inanimate object, but he was not a happy camper. I said later that night at the team meeting that Monty was getting a lot of heckling, but not to worry because he was deflecting it from the entire team. Unfortunately, it did not remain that way.

I sat down with Monty later just to let him know that if there was anything I could do, I would. He was still extremely cross, but determined to turn the events of the day to his advantage. 'This is going to make me play better, not worse,' he told me.

Back at the hotel it was on with the joggers and T-shirts and down to the team room to see what was happening. I had not set a time for the team meeting and just tried to catch everybody when they were not on their main course. We went through to the video room and shut the door to block out the girls' laughter.

There was a real feeling of excitement in the air, and everybody was on a high after what had been achieved. Having that kind of lead was from the land of dreams; I would have been happy with a reasonable start, just to have kept pace with them. To be four points ahead was nothing short of incredible.

Professionals do not go through rounds together as thoroughly as amateurs tend to, because if someone starts a bit too early in the day's play he is invariably asked, 'What happened on the eighteenth?' But that night there was plenty of chat about putts which had dropped and shots which had been decisive. There was a distinct buzz about the place.

I was able to continue the mood of the camp, kicking things off by saying, 'Don't forget: if you have two putts for a hole, take them.' Everybody was word-perfect on that one by now. I told them that if I missed the end of a match and they wondered why I was not there, then I would have a very good reason: I would either be on a short hole giving clubs to players or rushing to the clubhouse to get a tuna sandwich with no lumps for Monty. Just in case they had not noticed, I told them the flags were orange in the morning and red in the afternoon, but on a far more serious note I also pointed out that the crowds were just starting to say a few uncomplimentary things and not to let it affect them. If they could identify a miscreant then they were to try to get him or her removed by the marshals (although the way that particular breed behaved themselves on the Sunday, they were more likely to take any wrongdoers away and buy them a beer). I also reminded them that 6–2 seemed a big lead, but things could change rapidly. They had done a great job, better than we could have hoped for, but there was still a huge amount of work to do and we needed to grind it out for every point.

It was just a short meeting, and at the end of it Monty told the guys what was being said and that it was a problem, but to try to make it work for them and use it as a motivation. The response was that they could cope with anything.

Apart from groaning whenever I told them to use two putts if necessary, the players were pretty good at team meetings. Everybody chipped in where necessary so it was not just a question of my standing up and spouting off. Sam was never slow to offer his observations, and Monty and Olly usually had a word or two, but I did not have to call for order too often. The guys liked a quick meeting, and I wanted to go through the entire week without there being any whispering in corners. Whether or not the decisions I took were the right ones is ultimately debatable, as is everything you do as a captain, but I was fairly sure the players felt I was being totally open with them and keeping them informed about absolutely everything that was happening. It was a point which was very important to me.

Most of the players had to be up at 6 a.m. the following morning, so at about 9.30 p.m. they started drifting off to their rooms, while the Gang of Six reflected on the day's play over a nice glass of chilled Sauvignon Blanc. We were all relaxed. A score of 6–2 was the stuff of dreams. No one would have believed they could do that.

9 Second Helping

I T WOULD HAVE BEEN MADNESS not to go with the first-day line-up at the start of the second. There was too much risk involved in doing anything other than staying faithful to the guys who had performed so well in the previous day's foursomes – a format which has proved to be one of our perennial Achilles' heels. We had a healthy lead going into a rainy Saturday morning, but I was all too aware that without doing anything particularly wrong that scoreline could easily be reversed. The decision to stay as we were was, as I said, unanimous.

All decisions were taken well in advance because we never had meetings in the morning, for several reasons. With people playing at different times or not at all, it meant the travel and eating arrangements were fragmented, but the principal reason was because when you have to play you need your mind focused on that, not on whether or not your underpants match your socks, or which horse is likely to win the 2.45 at Lingfield. And the guys definitely did not need me to tell them that if they had two putts for a hole, they had to take them. My only duty each morning was to be there just in case anybody wanted to know or ask anything.

There was not the same atmosphere when we arrived at the course on the Saturday morning. That could have had something to do with the rain, but was more likely because of the stuffing we had given the home team in the first afternoon's fourballs. Lee and Darren beating Tiger Woods and David Duval had been a massive psychological boost for the team, as had winning a couple of matches on the last hole, which is always a considerable accomplishment. Ben Crenshaw's overnight job had obviously been much harder than mine, and after the first day's performance he was forced to change his line-up yet again. Apart from Hal Sutton and Jeff Maggert again, the Americans sent out another set of new pairings. It was perhaps a little early for them to be classed desperation measures, but there was a lot of shuffling going on in a bid to get more out of the American players. What compounded their captain's problems was that it was not the way he was pairing them, but the way we were playing against them. We had produced some tremendous golf; the Americans, without doing anything particularly wrong, had simply been outgunned.

My captaincy during the match thus far had involved no form of controversy. Although I obviously wanted that state of affairs to continue, the first indication that it might not came in the morning matches when Colin Montgomerie and Paul Lawrie faced Maggert and Sutton. We were on the green at the par five fourteenth and it was the Americans' turn to putt, but although one of them had marked the ball, it was the other who replaced it. Neither Paul nor Monty was certain if such an action was within the rules, and when I was asked I had to admit it was not something I had encountered before. Monty asked me to find out, and I thought, 'Oh my God.' My heart sank a little bit as I considered the possibility that this might cause an international incident, but a quick call to John Paramor on the walkie-talkie and I was assured it was perfectly legitimate in foursomes. By the time I found out the players had all teed off at the next hole anyway, so I am not sure we could have done anything about it even if the Americans had fallen foul of the rules.

The competition was spoiled by the weather for a time, and it was then that a radio reporter decided to test my patience with one of the many in-depth questions directed at me throughout the week. 'Will the rain benefit the Europeans more than the Americans?' I was asked. 'Yes,' I replied. 'But only if one of the Americans drowns.' Sometimes I wonder where they think them up.

Although there had been a rain delay, the deadline for the afternoon pairings was not put back and they had to be decided by 11.45 a.m. It was the hardest decision of the week because I wanted to give a chance to the three who had not yet played, but the way the pairings had worked out thus far offered me the opportunity, should I stick with them, of taking a big lead into the singles. I felt that that fact could not be ignored, no matter how tempting it was to give Andrew, Jean and Jarmo some action. I just could not afford to leave out Monty and Paul, and Sergio and Jesper, who were proving very tough combinations, or Lee and Darren, who accounted for Woods and Duval last time out, not to mention Mechanico, who was in great form and was Olly's ideal partner. Had the results been worse, it would have been easier to switch things around, but as it was there was no way I could make wholesale changes.

The only slight question mark was over Jesper, and I spoke with him going up the fourteenth fairway. He was a little undecided as to whether he wanted to play all five series. 'If you don't want to play, that's fine,' I told him. 'But you're playing well, you're a great pair, and if it is not going to be a big problem then I think you should play.' Almost immediately Jesper said, 'OK, I'll play.'

With that settled, I needed to tell the three who would miss out again, and give the reasons for their omission. It was a very difficult job, as usual. I saw Jean on the range where he was getting ready to play, and although I sensed his disappointment he still remained extremely supportive, and that was the most important thing. Andrew and Jarmo, who I found in the team room, suffered similar emotions, but also accepted the situation without complaint. They knew the decisions I had made had not been taken lightly, only after very careful consideration and taking advice. They might not have liked what I was doing, but they could certainly understand it.

Later that day, Andrew met up with Jarmo at the door of the team room and asked him if he was disappointed. The question drew a unique response. 'Do not use the word disappointed,' said Jarmo. 'I am a soldier, and when my commander orders me I will charge.' He then set off down the corridor full pelt. It was another example of Jarmo's mind working in mysterious ways.

Once the afternoon pairings were in the bag there was no going back – not that I would have wanted to. An indication of just how much the Americans were feeling the pressure, both from us and from their supporters, came in the first match of the afternoon, another new American pairing of Phil Mickelson and Tom Lehman facing Lee and Darren. There was an incident between the two pairs during the match, and how it managed to avoid getting to the press room I shall never know, but somehow the incident escaped the journalists' attention, otherwise much might have been made of it.

After the tenth had been finished, Lee and Darren hit a few putts, as most people do, while the Americans walked away to the next tee, where Mickelson drove off. It was a clear breach of golfing etiquette, because you should not drive off until your opponents have joined you on the tee. Lee and Darren walked on to the eleventh and stood around, because it was not their honour, and eventually enquired of the Americans, 'Are you going to hit?' to which Mickelson replied, 'I have.' Lee looked at him and said in a surprised voice, 'Oh, have you?' My players were extremely miffed indeed. They thought it a tremendous breach of etiquette, but I thought it should remain under wraps. Lee was particularly annoyed. He, like most players in the world, is a stickler for course etiquette and rules, but I was worried that had we made a fuss the Americans might have put in a counter-claim, stating that we should not have been practice-putting when they were already on the next tee. Also, I had asked the PGA of America to do something about practice-putting after a hole had been finished. I thought I might leave myself open to charges of hypocrisy if I kicked up a fuss, so I decided against it. Whatever the rights and wrongs of the situation, it was a clear indication that if these things were not watched closely they could get out of control.

Not being sure if the incident would stay inside the ropes, I went to find Ben. I told him I thought something like that might happen, but that if the press got hold of it I would play it down and not say a lot. Ben agreed, and we decided that rather than make anything of it, the best decision would be to let it rest. Ironically, someone had asked at a team meeting earlier in the week if it was OK to drive if Americans were still practice-putting on the previous green. The problem was not a new one, and I have felt in the past there should be a limit on the length of time anybody can practise after a hole has been finished.

A bigger worry for me was the length of time my players were out on the course. Every match went to at least the seventeenth green, and two went all the way. Had we lost one 5 & 4 and won another by the same margin, the players would have been slightly less tired going into Sunday. The second afternoon is always very tense because it not only determines how the teams will stand going into the singles, but also the order you send them out in.

I know how the pressure builds on a Saturday afternoon, and I have never forgotten an incident during a fourball match at the Belfry in 1989. Howard Clark and I were up against Curtis Strange and Payne Stewart, and ours was the last match out. Whether or not we went into the last day with a lead depended on the outcome. We were on the seventeenth green, having squared the match at the previous hole, and we both had putts to win the hole. Howard was six feet away and I was just inside him, but we decided that I should go first because neither of us liked the look of the putts, and mine was more straightforward. It made sense, because it meant I could relax a bit more; had Howard gone first and missed, the pressure would really have been on.

I felt perfectly all right until I took my stance, and then the most peculiar thing happened. It was a unique experience, and one which I am delighted to say has never been repeated. I decided it was an inside left putt, took a couple of practice swings, moved up to the ball and placed the putter head behind it. I was just about to shuffle my feet and steady myself when I realised I was paralysed from the hips down. I was so nervous I could not move my feet at all. The only thing I could think was, 'What the f*** do I do now?' I wanted to walk away and compose myself, but I could not budge an inch. All I could do was point my shoulders in the right direction and hope it did the trick. I finally managed to take the putter head back and strike the ball, and although it was not a good putt it dribbled in the left edge and we were one up going down the last. Only then did any feeling return to my legs, and even then I did not feel in total control of them. It was the most pressure I have ever felt on a golf course, and I would not experience anything similar until Oak Hill six years later.

I was perfectly aware that my players would be experiencing similar emotions as we grinded away on that long afternoon, but Paul Lawrie looked to be in total control. The pressure and the crowd had absolutely no influence on him, and he played his normal game. A lot of us on tour wish we had that kind of temperament, but it is obviously something you either have or you do not have. It served Paul splendidly on his Ryder Cup debut, and will continue to do so in the many I expect him to play in the future.

The point he and Monty gained against Tiger Woods and Steve Pate was huge in every respect. The USA had thrown a lot of good golf at us and we were in the process of trying to build a wall to stop them breaking through. Their point was a very big part of that barrier. Monty's performance all week had been enormous on and off the course. He was a figure the players looked up to, and I and my assistants were all too happy to confide in him. His performance had been nothing less than we anticipated, an integral part of the success we had enjoyed up to that point.

It was an equally brilliant performance by Olly and Mechanico to squeeze a half out of Leonard and Sutton. Miguel had produced extremely solid golf, and the two shots he hit into the eighteenth were right out of the middle of the bat. I could not have asked for more from him; I had worked him hard and he had responded magnificently.

We were a trifle less hot than on the opening day, but through sheer guts, determination and no little talent we lost neither ground nor face. The run of the ball was not as much with us either, but still it was not going for the USA much. By the end of the day there had been four series and we had not been beaten in any, which would have been a marvellous achievement on home soil, never mind away. A lead going into the final day was no less than we deserved, and more than we could have hoped for arriving in Boston. There would be no over-confidence, though, no room for gloating. Our attention had to be devoted to the twelve singles matches which would decide the outcome.

Day 2 Morning Foursomes

Match 9: Colin Montgomerie/Paul Lawrie v. Hal Sutton/Jeff Maggert

Sutton and Maggert had proved themselves the toughest of the USA's first-day pairings, and we knew they would have every intention of enhancing their reputations against our lead-off pair. They would have to do it from behind though, because Monty's magnificent five-iron tee shot to the short second finished ten feet away, close enough for Paul to select the right line from left of the flag and produce a winning birdie.

This was a real sluggers match: whatever one hit the other with, the response was similar. Long before it reached that stage, it was obviously a match which would finish much closer to home than out in the country. Indeed, it went all the way.

An indication of the kind of stick Monty was receiving from the crowd came on the sixth after Sutton coaxed in a fifteen-footer to put the European number one under pressure. Monty had a six-footer for a half, but just as he was about to take the putter head back an idiot yelled at him. Monty backed away, glared, settled, and then drilled the ball home before staring in the general direction of the troublemaker, without ever once losing self-control. 'These people are too stupid to understand that that type of thing only serves to make me more determined,' he said later.

After falling behind, it took the Americans seven more holes to draw level, Monty and Paul unable to match their birdie on the par five ninth. Only two more holes were needed for the USA to take the lead, but it reverted to all square again on the twelfth when Sutton and Maggert followed our bogey of the previous hole, when we failed to get up and down from a greenside bunker, with one of their own.

The standard of play, though, was outstanding, and when both birdied fifteen, it looked like nothing would separate the sides. The seventeenth would prove to be our undoing, however; an American birdie there proved crucial. Maggert rammed in the ball from 25 feet to put his side dormie one up. Monty and Sutton both put their partners in good positions off the tee at the last, but Paul's body language said everything about an approach shot that finished some twenty yards away, while Maggert's towering seven iron came down like an arrow through our hearts, stopping just two feet from the hole.

The Americans were three under par for the last four holes and still won only by the narrowest of margins.

USA win 1 up

Match 10: Lee Westwood/Darren Clarke v. Jim Furyk/Mark O'Meara

Lee, who had enjoyed the experience of playing with Nick Faldo in Valderrama on his debut, and Darren, who had benefited from one match with Colin Montgomerie there, had taken great pride in beating Woods and Duval the previous afternoon, and I felt confident they would still be on a high and ready to increase their points haul no matter who the opposition was. It was another new American pairing facing them, one which featured two of the world's best putters. Thankfully, it would be a day when their blades remained cold and their faces reflected their fortunes, while my boys looked as if they were enjoying every minute of it.

Neither pair made the fastest of starts. It would be a case of grinding for glory rather than shooting the lights out of a course which had proved itself a true test. It rewarded good play and penalised anything sloppy, while making demands of every club in the bag. Dropped shots rarely meant anything but the loss of a hole – a fact the two Europeans discovered early on in the match, but their first birdie of the round on the sixth brought the match back to its starting position. We took a lead we would never lose on the ninth with a second birdie, and from that moment on there was a palpable air of confidence surrounding the two friends. They looked and played as if they were in control, even though their play was more solid than spectacular.

A terrific chip over a bunker by Lee on the par four twelfth put us two up, and Darren's six-footer on the fourteenth green put us three ahead and within sight of another point. After two more halves the players shook hands. It was good to get something on the board at the start of the day.

'What a boost that was,' said Lee, who is likely to form a formidable partnership with the big Ulsterman

for many Ryder Cups to come. 'Our on-course chemis-
try is very good,' Darren said. 'We just went out and had
a few laughs. The Americans did not see the joke.'

Europe win 3 & 2

Match 11: Miguel Angel Jiménez/Padraig Harrington v. Steve Pate/Tiger Woods

The USA had been searching – in vain for the most part, both here and at Valderrama – for somebody to link up with Woods in either fourballs or foursomes. Despite an impressive amateur matchplay record which produced three US titles, then two majors plus the world number one spot since turning professional, his Ryder Cup record did not match. Prior to tee-off here he had one point from seven starts, and on the first day he had played well but lost both matches. Steve Pate had been called up to help improve that record, and there were early signs that the USA had finally found a partner for Woods. Birdie, birdie, birdie, and we were three down without having done anything particularly wrong.

One of the messages I had hammered home all week in team meetings covered what to do when falling behind. 'Stick in there, hit fairways and greens, keep the pressure on and you never know what might happen.' My boys had obviously been paying attention. Neither the Spaniard nor the Irishman ever show much outward evidence of distress, no matter what emotions they have to deal with inside; if they ever brandished a white towel it would be to wipe clubs with, not to wave in surrender. Slowly, but impressively, they chipped and putted away at the deficit, although their recovery started on the basis of securing a half rather than a win.

Padraig matched the USA's fourth successive birdie on the fourth to stop the rot, and further improvement quickly followed the short rain delay. By the turn we had pulled the Americans back to just one hole. The lead vanished completely when Woods and Pate failed to make par on eleven, and a match worthy of anything that had gone before was developing.

The pivotal hole proved to be the fourteenth, and it needed an eagle for the Americans to win it. We had four holes left to try to get something out of the match, but each was halved.

'We knew coming down the stretch we needed this point to have a chance,' admitted Woods. Padraig could not hide his disappointment at coming so close after weathering the opening storm. His sadness was understandable after a cruel piece of luck on the seventeenth when he hit what looked like a perfect approach, only to see the ball stop one roll short of hitting a slope which would have taken it down to the hole. 'That was robbery,' he said afterwards. 'I couldn't believe it when the ball stopped. It would have been stone dead had it rolled back. You need to get some breaks, and seventeen went against us. To halve the match would have been a big bonus.'

So Woods and Pate survived to take a point and make sure the USA's first-day deficit was not made worse after day two.

USA win 1 up

Match 12: Jesper Parnevik/Sergio Garcia v. Payne Stewart/Justin Leonard

Americans do like a handle, and our boys were christened The Kid and The Lid – Sergio, the youngest Ryder Cup player ever, for obvious reasons, and Jesper because of the upturned peak on his baseball cap. Sergio had already proved himself a star of today rather than tomorrow with his first-day performances – rarely can a debut have been more glittering – and Jesper was ideal alongside him, knowing when to let the teenager off the leash and when to bring him to heel. I knew it would take something special to beat them, and Stewart and Leonard were unable to find it.

Both sides, particularly the Americans, found out how damaging bogeys can be when they traded the first two holes, but the match quickly settled after that, a first birdie of the day for my pair on six enough to give them the lead.

This encounter would be decided around the turn, where Jesper and Sergio prospered through their own brilliance and a little American benevolence. Birdies won both the ninth and tenth holes, and a Stewart and Leonard bogey on eleven meant we had our biggest advantage of any match so far. The home side had five over-par returns in their first eleven holes, and at this level scoring like that is fatal. And so it proved.

Four up was reduced to three by a rare American birdie on thirteen, and although they repeated the feat on the next, so did we. Two more pars were good enough to secure victory, the match over when Stewart could not make a six-footer disappear.

It was Jesper who had put a collar round the team's neck with the name 'underpuppies' on it, but he was aware that puppies can have their day every bit as much as dogs of war. He and Sergio were producing golf of a ferocious nature, dangerous to anybody coming within range. 'I think the fans seem to like us,' said Sergio. Not as much as he liked Jesper, though. 'I'm just so confident knowing that my partner will always make good putts and shots.' Jesper returned the compliment. 'Every time I needed Sergio he was right there.'

Europe win 3 & 2

Afternoon Fourballs

Match 13: Lee Westwood/Darren Clarke v. Phil Mickelson/Tom Lehman

The USA had failed to make any inroads into our four-point lead during the morning session, a series neither Mickelson nor Lehman played any part in, while my boys were still hungry for work and points.

Mickelson had decided after a hard time on the greens on the day before that a change of putter was needed. It also changed his luck, but, thankfully, none of their team members responded to the early initiative swing. Indeed, this would be the only full point Ben's side won all afternoon.

It quickly became obvious it was going to be hard work to get anything as Mickelson birdied the third, the eighth also producing another American success. The tenth would prove another good one for home supporters, Mickelson producing the shot of the match: a wedge from about the 100-yard mark landing softly and finishing within tap-in range. What it meant to the Americans was shown when Lehman gave his partner a hug. It would not be the last time that weekend he would wear his emotions on his sleeve.

At three down, it was going to take something extra special to turn this one round in our favour. It was a quality of the entire team that no matter the odds against them there would be no surrender. Lee and Darren would never stop fighting; there is no such thing in their eyes as a lost cause, but this time their determination would go unrewarded. We just could not find the birdies when we needed them most. Lee's two at the sixteenth was too little too late, because by this time the Americans were dormie three needing just one half from the last three holes. It came on the seventeenth.

USA win 2 & 1

Match 14: Jesper Parnevik/Sergio Garcia v. Davis Love III and David Duval

If any match looked capable of producing a rash of red on the scoreboard, then this had to be among the favourites. Nobody was disappointed with the number of birdies on offer, with an eagle thrown in for good measure. It was a classic duel.

America were two up after four and level after six. It was that kind of a match, with Sergio running, jumping and skipping around, even finding time to give Ben Crenshaw's wife Julie a kiss during the heat of battle. Sergio's birdie on the eighth gave us the lead for the first time, but it lasted just as long as it took Love to eagle the par five ninth. Duval's birdie on ten was then immediately nullified by Jesper's on the eleventh, and the same pair repeated the exchange on thirteen and fourteen. It was nothing short of scintillating.

The match looked as if it would swing the USA's way when their birdie on the sixteenth was not equalled. Then the two pairs took to the final tee. Cometh the hour, cometh the boy; up stepped Sergio to produce three of the best shots of the week. A massive drive left him just 155 yards, then a towering eight iron saw his ball finish just eight feet from the hole. It had to be converted to halve the match, and Sergio knew long before it dropped where it was heading.

Scottish golf writer Alister Nicol summed Sergio up perfectly when he wrote:

'What a wonderful gift he is to the game of golf. His enthusiasm, his sheer joy, his knack for producing shots of stunning quality just have to be good for the future of European golf. He's a natural crowd-pleaser whose antics endear rather than enrage. He is a kid with genuine superstar quality.'

'That was the biggest putt of my professional career,' Sergio said afterwards, before proving just how much he was enjoying himself by adding, 'But I hope to make a bigger one tomorrow.' Jesper was almost speechless. 'What can I say about Sergio?'

Match halved

Match 15: *José Maria Olazábal/Miguel Angel Jiménez v. Justin Leonard/Hal Sutton*

Sutton, who had won two out of three with Maggert and been the rather surprising mainstay of the American team, was given former Open champion and Carnoustie runner-up Leonard as his afternoon partner. It was another physically and mentally draining match which, like many before it, went the distance. Every single encounter so far had gone to show just why the Ryder Cup is now one of the biggest events in golf, if not the biggest. It throws up so much drama, and this match would prove no exception.

There could be no doubting who was the senior partner of the two Spaniards, as Miguel stroked in three successive birdies on four, five and six to take us from one down to two up, a position we enjoyed until Leonard birdied the ninth. The Americans spent most of the day playing catch-up but only succeeded in keeping pace, until the sixteenth brought a change of fortune. Sutton's six iron, it has to be conceded, was superb, landing a couple of inches from the hole and guaranteeing a winning birdie. It squared the match, and the teams were inseparable right to the last putt, which was a crucial par-saver by Mechanico, the hero of the match.

'I feel very emotional,' he said afterwards. 'I feel very tired now, but after getting that half I now feel I can play twice tomorrow,' he added. Olly was typically quick to praise his partner, a player I felt had been underestimated by the Americans, but who had shown himself capable of golf of the highest quality.

Match halved

Match 16: Colin Montgomerie/Paul Lawrie v. Steve Pate/Tiger Woods

If anything was likely to fire up Monty (and he needs very little stoking), the sight of Woods across the tee from him had every chance. Of the many huge performances the world number three has produced at the top level, this was right up there with the best – a fact his playing partner acknowledged afterwards. Monty was nothing short of awesome, his putter so hot it is a wonder his fingers were not soldered to it by the end of a match which added yet more glitter to an already sparkling competition.

No fewer than five birdies had been thrown at the Americans by the sixteenth tee, but such was the quality hurled back that we were just one ahead. Paul had sat back in admiration of his partner, but had obviously been inspired by the demonstration, and proved it on the short sixteenth. His tee shot ended no more than a foot from the pin, and that made us dormie two. A half on the seventeenth was enough for another big point.

'I holed some key putts when I had to, and then Paul finished things off,' said Monty, who added that the fourteenth hole had been a key point of the match. He had come up short with two drivers, but Woods had found the green with a four iron with his second. 'That's a hell of an advantage, but when he missed his eagle putt and I managed to get up and down for birdie, I felt confident we were going to win.' Monty produced six birdies in a near flawless display neither of the Americans could match. 'It's frustrating when you play well and still lose,' said Tiger. Welcome to the Ryder Cup.

Europe win 2 & 1

USA 6 EUROPE 10

Whatever high we were on going into the team room, I knew we had to come down quickly in order to decide the order of the following day's play. This, more than any other series, was a group thing, and was far from easy. The three guys who had not played at all wanted to tee off pretty early, and everybody could understand that. I was happy to accommodate them, because no one would feel at ease going off nine, ten, eleven or twelve and possibly having to come down the last with the entire match depending on the result.

But I was reluctant to put the three rookies at one, two and three because it did not take a nuclear physicist to work out that Ben would load the front with his big guns. He had no choice: had he not done so and got off to a bad start then the whole thing could have been over before the big boys had had a chance to do anything about it. We had to decide how to respond to that, and we opted to send out the rookies earlyish, with the majority of our better players towards the end. If matches were tight and full of pressure, then they would be best equipped, having played so well all through the year and that week, to deal with it.

There was more input from the players at that meeting than at any other. Ultimately it was my decision, but I like to think I am more of a democrat than an autocrat and I was willing to listen to and take on board anything they thought was important. I wanted to know what was going on in their heads, keeping my finger on the pulse all the way through.

Because Lee is a fairly brisk player we thought that letting him go off first would be a good idea. Darren is no slowcoach, either so the two of them going off first and second was something they would relish, as well as allowing us to slip in the new boys immediately afterwards. They were happy at three, four and five in whatever order, and had no problems about facing any of the opposition, even though it was likely to be the best American players.

It was then a question of organising the rest, and there was not a huge amount of discussion. We put Monty at number ten, because we felt that if we were going to win then it would be round about there where it would all be decided. Paul was more than happy to go out last and, I suspect, was hoping that he would need to come up eighteen and win the hole to secure a European triumph. He really was that keen to be in a pressure situation, and I was perfectly content. Put him in those situations, as he had shown at the Open and during the week in Boston, and he was cool and rock-solid. Sergio was also perfectly happy at eleven so that he could have a lie-in, be off late and hopefully have the putt that decided the match.

So we had our start and finish, and the other four slotted in nicely in the middle, in no particular order.

There were quite a lot of questions about individuals and their performances at the end-of-day press conference, and I was pleased to be able to say in public just how proud I was of every member of the team, even those who had not played, because they had contributed to the spirit and atmosphere and had accepted that the way I was doing things was for the greater good. They had known our thoughts and game plan every step of the way, and had been totally supportive. I had arrived in Boston with the objectives of getting 100 per cent out of the team and the most points I could. I felt we had gone about it in the right way.

Although aware of some of the things which had been happening behind the ropes, making any kind of issue out of it would not have been in our best interests. We had known on arrival that there would be big crowds, and most would be supporting the home team. I sensed the press might be trying to whip something up in this area, so I tried to play it as carefully as I could. Upsetting local sensitivities would never help our cause. There had been heckling, yes, but some of the Americans had also come in for criticism. 'I would describe the crowd as frisky and wouldn't say they were ill-mannered or anything like that,' I said, although at the same time aware that Monty might take issue with me on that perspective. 'I think the crowds have been very fair and we have been enjoying their company,' I added. Nothing there they could use against us tomorrow, I thought.

I was asked how big was the point Monty and Paul got in the final fourballs against Tiger Woods and Steve Pate, and was pleased to report it had been a huge one. 'They had thrown a lot of good golf at us and we were in the process of trying to put up a wall and stop them breaking through,' I said. 'That point was a very big factor in that wall and Colin's contribution this week has been enormous. He is certainly an integral factor in the success we've enjoyed so far this week.' The point was not lost on American captain Ben Crenshaw either, who spoke glowingly about Monty. 'He's a wonderful golfer in every way. He's shown it many times in many places and he certainly lifts the players with him. You could say a lot of things about him, but he's a tremendous golfer.'

It was a pleasure for me to be able to pay tribute to the play of the Americans, because they had made no small contribution to what had been a feast of outstanding golf. There were two very good teams out there playing very well under pressure, and it was a shame one would have to lose (although the possibility of a tie did enter the equation).

Not a day went by without there being one or two questions about Sergio, and I reiterated what I had said about him being a replacement for the young Seve – a charismatic force with a hugely positive effect on the team. Only a few minutes earlier, in the team room, he had been with the others watching the Golf Channel when they showed a clip of him. He had gathered all the others together, saying, 'Look at this next hole, watch this, watch this!' But they skipped elsewhere and did not show what Sergio wanted them to see, so he started throwing things at the screen. 'Livewire' seemed an apt description of the teenager.

There was a need for extra caution in my reply when the anticipated question about whether or not I expected to win from this position surfaced. The last thing we needed to be hit with on Sunday morning were the 'we're going to win it' headlines. But I did admit I would be disappointed if we did not, because a four-point lead was a reasonable one, although we were under no illusions about how hard the Americans would come back at us. 'I'll be tucking the boys in with a glass of milk, saying, "Get a good night's sleep, we have work to do tomorrow," ' I said.

Later, a very happy and contented bunch of players made their way back to the hotel for a relaxing evening. Everybody would enjoy not having to be up at 6 a.m. so, free of that restriction at last, we were able to spend a little longer than normal over dinner. As we gathered for that evening's meeting, not one person in that room would have predicted a few days ago that we would be going into the final day with a four-point lead, but this is what we had. It had been a brilliant performance around a course which, if anything, suited their players more than ours.

The team meeting was a little later than normal and only started after I had had to hunt for Sergio. I was getting a little worried because he had not brought that night's homework for me to mark. When I knocked on his door a young man in his early twenties answered, which I thought a bit odd, but when he opened it further I could see Sergio lying on his front over a table with a towel over his backside, so I assumed he was having a massage. He jumped up as if he knew he should be somewhere else, but I told him not to rush, just to come through when he was ready.

The slight delay enabled Mechanico to continue his habit of a lifetime and eat his dinner slowly and meticulously. He had looked at the wine list at the beginning of the week, filed away a few favourites mentally, and then enjoyed his meal-time tasting sessions. While we all shovelled down our food, sat back and patted our bellies, Miguel gradually worked through the courses with a look of pleasure and contentment on his face after every mouthful. He was wiping away the last crumbs from the corner of his mouth when his fellow Spaniard graced us with his presence.

There were only a few things to run through. If I was not on the first tee when their match went off then it would be because I was relaying clubs on the second hole, not because I was in the clubhouse sipping a Budweiser. And then I bellowed, 'And if you have two putts for a hole, then f***ing use them,' just in time before being drowned in a sea of heckling. It was my last chance to dispense this wisdom, so I made sure I emphasised it.

I also warned them to watch out for intimidation towards the end, to be ready to cope with anything. As soon as I told them under no circumstances to react to the crowd, Monty turned to Jarmo and said, 'No guns.' It was a reference to the match the Swede had had against Phil Mickelson during an Alfred Dunhill Cup match at St Andrews. After several birdie putts, Jarmo had pretended his putter was a shotgun and had fired into the sky, an act the American had taken exception to. Jarmo insisted there would be no repetition, and said, 'There will be no problem. I will just put my arms in the air and say, "I love you, I love you all." ' (The irony was not lost on anybody when the singles draw threw Jarmo and Mickelson together, but there was not the slightest hint of bad blood the next day and the American publicly congratulated his opponent afterwards for his sportsmanship during their match.)

I also thought it important to remind them that they had been playing in fourballs and slowly for five days, and to be careful when it was just head-to-head and at a different pace, and not to rush. I told them they had done a great job for the first two days and I could not have asked for more. If they continued to play the way they had then they would win the match. They were told to forget the leaderboards and not to count points already gathered. 'Just concentrate on your own match and try to make it the one that secures our win,' I said. There is always the danger, if you start counting up points and think you have enough, that you relax too much and lose a match where you could have secured a vital half.

I did not say anything special to those who had not played because they had been privy to everything throughout the week. They were just keen to get some action after what had been a difficult, if not unprecedented, time for them.

Most players went to their rooms between ten and eleven, while Ken, Sam and I put the day to bed in normal fashion with a glass of chilled dry white. We knew we were on the verge of a victory few outside the team room had considered possible before we arrived. We also knew just how fickle a game golf can be, and how quickly fortunes can swing. We were determined only to celebrate when another four and a half points had been added to our scoresheet.

What we did not know, and could not have guessed, was that we were in for the ugliest day in the game's history. It was the day the Ryder Cup almost died of shame, a day sporting America should be thoroughly ashamed of. We knew we were in for a tough battle, but we never realised we were entering what former Royal & Ancient secretary Sir Michael Bonallack aptly described as 'scenes resembling a bear pit'.

10 Enter the Bears

THE FINAL MORNING ALLOWED us the luxury of the only lie-in of the week, a well earned rest for tired muscles. I took breakfast along with the early starters. The players were looking forward to getting the job done and the mood was positive, enthusiastic and confident.

The general atmosphere when I arrived at the course about half an hour before the first match was due off was slightly higher-octane than on the first two days, but still there was nothing to suggest what was about to unfold. The crowd seemed to be pretty normal and there was not a sniff of hostility in the air. I stood by the putting green, conveniently placed about ten yards from the first tee, chatting to a few people, before Lee Westwood and Tom Lehman arrived from the practice range to start the day's proceedings.

Ben Crenshaw's obsession with golfing history seemed to have crossed new boundaries when I saw his side's last-day uniform for the first time. I thought they were wearing photograph albums, not shirts. Apparently, Ben had delved into the photo archives and pulled out pictures of winning American teams. They were then turned into a montage on which the design of the shirt was based. To me, the shirts exemplified the difference in dress taste between our two continents. Suffice to say, had I laid out anything similar in front of my team on the final morning, I would have been asked to seek therapy, or been thrown in the harbour.

It was at that point, hours before the horrors on the seventeenth green forever labelled the day the worst in the competition's history, that I first became aware that things were not as they should be. It seemed that the Americans had decided that if they were going to whip our backsides then they would have to whip up the crowd. Tom Lehman started it. He came to the tee fairly late to be greeted by a loud cheer and shouts of encouragement. When the noise subsided the faint strains of 'God Bless America' could be heard, sung by a handful of people standing on a small knoll some fifty yards from the tee. It died away completely after a while, but Lehman decided to milk every last drop out of the moment. Although the singing had stopped, he walked over towards them and started trying to encourage them into an encore. He then began conducting, waving his arms around like a dervish. Before you could say God Bless America he had the entire crowd singing it again, just a minute before tee-off time.

Lehman's behaviour was not only unnecessary, but also extremely bad manners. I had always thought he had a bit more about him than to descend to that level of behaviour. It was most peculiar. Occasionally you see players working with the crowd, but nothing like that, and certainly nothing like what we had to experience for the rest of the day. As Bernard and Lesley Gallacher wrote to Jane and me afterwards: 'The matches will probably recover, but the scars will remain for a very long time. We were shocked by the hostility of the final day, but to your eternal credit, you both maintained your integrity and perspective when your hosts completely lost the plot.'

Whatever plot Lehman had in mind was definitely one which did not belong on a golf course. I do not know if the Boston Pops conductor had gone to his head on the Wednesday night, but he was certainly acting out of character. As soon as he had teed off I looked at Lee, and he fixed me with a gaze which suggested amazement at what was happening. Although totally unflappable, even at the worst of times, he raised his eyebrows as if to say, 'What on earth is he doing?' We were shocked because Lehman had always been fairly quiet and laid back.

I followed the pair until they reached the second so that I knew what Lee was hitting on the first of the short holes and could report back to those following. As soon as he hit I dropped back and saw Darren chip in at the first against Hal Sutton to give us the first blood of the day. I wondered if it might be an omen. Sam went back to wander up the first with the three who had not played before, and I went with them as much as I could. We had correctly guessed that the Americans would put most of the heavy artillery out first because they had no option, but Jarmo Sandelin, Jean Van de Velde and Andrew Coltart were not in the least bit fazed about facing three of their best players. If they were going to face anybody, then why not Woods, Love and Mickelson? They would not lack for support. My assistants could even go right up to them and talk – there was no restriction on that. It was only in the area of giving advice that they were handcuffed. Sam opted not to get too close anyway, just to let the boys know that there was somebody out there pulling for them. With twelve matches out there rather than just four, our armbands, guaranteeing inside-the-ropes access, were spread a little more thinly, but I wanted to ensure every match had some backing.

The Sandelin–Mickelson pairing, as I have mentioned, had its own not-so-hidden agenda because of previous events, and it looked like the crowd were aware of the history between them as early as the second hole. Jarmo hit a wonderful shot to about two feet, and once he got to the green he put his hands in his pockets and started looking around. The crowd, thinking he was looking at Mickelson and expecting the putt to be conceded, started booing. What they did not realise was that Jarmo had developed a hole in one of his pockets and had lost the coin he marks his ball with. For most people that would not be a problem, but to Jarmo it could upset his equilibrium quite easily. Using his own money was out of the question, so he went to the crowd to try to scrounge some shrapnel before returning to the green to mark. He then taped up the pocket with elastoplast so he could put his marker back in there. He could not put it in the other pocket because that was not normal routine for him. And people think Jesper Parnevik is eccentric.

Sam walked the front nine with Jarmo while Ken checked the pins to see if anybody was having trouble putting to them. Anything he spotted came back to me so that I could pass on the information. Once I had done all the clubs for the second, I went off to do the same with the seventh, where Lee and Darren both hit seven irons when previously it had been a three. The players knew one another's distances, so information like that could prove very valuable, especially considering the difference Sunday's conditions had made to club selection.

It was at about this point, when the first match was through eight holes, that I joined Jesper playing against David Duval. They were on the fourth fairway and a huge leaderboard there was painting a picture I did not care for in the slightest. There was a sea of USA red, and it was not my favourite colour. I remember thinking to myself: 'What on earth can I do to reverse this?' If a captain did have any power to change anything, this would be the time to exercise it. Now was the time to bring my Superman cape out of the bag, put it on and fly to the rescue. I discussed it with chauffeur Coops and we did not have any brainwaves; we decided I should just carry on doing what I had been doing all week: getting the clubs to the players and telling them to stick with their opponents and hopefully get a reward for their persistence.

Just looking at that scoreboard was one of the week's least pleasurable moments, and, apart from having to speak to those who were not playing, there had been few so far. It would be a total understatement to say I had a sinking feeling. We were rapidly going under, and nobody seemed to be throwing any lifejackets our way. We were not just one or two down in two or three matches, but two or three down in five or six matches – a world of difference. I could see our four-point lead disappearing in the first five matches. (I was wrong: it went in the first four.)

The first four matches in particular looked bad news, but Andrew Coltart was hanging on to Tiger Woods and playing really well. The boys behind would get a real confidence boost if he could extend the world number one's run of less-than-impressive Ryder Cup results, but he was to become not only a victim of Woods, but also of an incredible incident on the ninth hole.

Andrew hit left off nine, and when he got down there to search for the ball a group of Americans said the ball had clattered into the trees and gone further in. Everybody looked some thirty to forty yards off the fairway, but nothing was found after five minutes and Andrew had to go back to play another ball. Just after it was too late to do anything about it, the ball was found plugged – incredible in itself – just six feet from the edge of the fairway. Nobody could prove that Andrew had been misdirected by the crowd, but it seemed strange that after he went back to play the other ball, a group of Americans started high-fiving one another and saying, 'Job well done.'

For a ball to be embedded it cannot have hit a tree, although the Americans said it definitely had. If it had hit a tree and was plugged, then somebody must have trod on it. The situation was one which should never happen under any circumstances. There was a definite atmosphere developing, and not a particularly nice one at that.

Sam and I went down to where the incident had happened and wondered what we could do about it. The answer was simple: nothing. A search for the ball had been conducted and it was declared lost. Hole over, no appeal. It was a serious blow, because Woods had chipped in minutes earlier for a slightly fortuitous win and was now two up and looking good, which was a lot more than could be said for us.

After that incident, I not only realised we were in the really deep stuff, but I started to get a bad feeling about what was happening outside as well as inside the ropes. The crowds were getting particularly noisy, especially when our players were about to hit their shots. A little bit of excitement is expected, but when somebody has called for quiet and it is their turn to hit, there should be silence. This was not the case here. This crowd was not one you would associate with golf. Repeatedly, silence was called for, but just as our boys were about to hit someone would call out from the throng. Now Americans might point out that this has happened before and that they were subjected to barracking like this at Valderrama. My response is that two wrongs do not make a right, and whatever happened in Spain was nowhere near as bad as it was in Boston. I have never had to use the word 'disgraceful' before when referring to golf galleries, but it was the only one which aptly described their behaviour. It was incredible.

Making a noise when players miss putts or hit into water or bunkers is one thing, but personal abuse is altogether different. We are going to get into a situation where fights will break out if we do not do something to stop standards declining. At one stage the atmosphere got so bad in Monty's match with Payne Stewart that his retired father had to leave the course because he could not take any more. The abuse hurled was vile, and included somebody yelling out, 'Monty, you're a fat c***!' It was heartbreaking, and how on earth Eimear managed to keep her composure I will never know.

Some of it was also premeditated. Tim Barter, a Sky golf commentator and Andrew's coach, was watching from behind the ropes when three guys muscled their way to the front and identified who was playing. 'It's Coltart,' said one, while another checked a notebook and said, 'Two waggles and then he takes the club back.' Tim could not believe it. They had been following our players in practice rounds making a list of all their different idiosyncrasies and pre-shot routines so that they knew exactly when to shout out to cause maximum harm. Tim threatened to have them thrown out if they did it again, and they said, 'You're just a sore loser,' which is, of course, and oddly enough, just what Davis Love said afterwards. It really does show up the mentality of that type of person.

As I said, the day was starting to get distasteful in every respect. I saw Sutton walking fifteen yards behind Darren at one stage in their match, pumping his fists and revving up the crowd. Maybe standards are changing, but that should not be part of golf. It was probably a good job for the American that he was behind Darren, because had he been seen performing his histrionic gestures, I do not think he would have enjoyed getting a thick ear from the big Ulsterman. On other occasions there were instances of people from the

official party willing our shots into water. Your opponent making a mistake is something you occasionally
might hope for inside, but actually to shout it out loud
is beyond belief. Golf is not gladiatorial and should
never be, but there seems to be a faction that wants it
to be put in that arena.

The rowdiness and disorder was by no means
restricted to the crowd. I saw marshals repeatedly turn
to the crowd and pump their fists in the air. Those who
were supposed to be controlling were actually inciting.
And when Andrew stood over one putt, some cretin
yelled out, 'Ya ain't gonna hole it, get off the course.'
The guy was identified and marshals removed him –
probably to give him a pat on the back. Like the
marshals, I had very little control over what was
happening either side of the ropes, but I was beginning
to think that there had to be a limit to the length of time
things would go the Americans' way.

One by one the results were registered on the board,
and for anybody from Europe they did not make happy
reading. Lee, Darren, Jarmo, Jean and Andrew all lost
before the seventeenth, and I was on the fourteenth
green when Jesper had to concede defeat to David
Duval. I have never seen anything quite like Duval's
reaction to the win; had I not known better, I would
have sworn the American was on something. Earlier in
the year he had shot a 59, and his salute when the last
putt dropped was brief and made with a single fist – and
he was probably embarrassed about doing that. But
here he was more animated than ever before in his
professional life, strutting around the green with a hand
cupped behind an ear. I have heard it suggested he was
responding to taunts earlier in the week and wondering
where they were now after he had won 5 & 4, but I do
not believe that. It was so incredible that I can only
suspect it was another instance of a deliberate attempt

to whip up the crowd. Whatever the reason, the galleries responded. It was ugly.

Fortunately we had a few guys out there looking as if they were capable of getting points for us. Padraig was doing well against O'Meara, Mechanico was holding up well against Pate, Olly was four clear of Leonard, Monty looked OK against Stewart and Paul was in control against Maggert. I could see where the points might come from, but it was going to be close – too close, perhaps. When you are not playing you do not need a degree in maths to work out the equation. It was not all bad, but at the halfway stage it was fairly evident it was going down to the wire. It was essential we got something out of Mechanico and Olly, because Sergio was not looking too comfortable against Furyk. I felt that Padraig, too, had to win.

Padraig is a master in a close situation, and I had a gut feeling he would come through, although he gave me one little heart flutter I had not anticipated. Having seen the top six matches all lose, I was concentrating my attention on the finishing holes, particularly the sixteenth, where I could give advice on what clubs had been used there. The hole was not as easy as it had been, with the pin cut front right and the wind coming in from that direction. Lee had used a seven iron, then Andrew elected to cut up a six, but it was not such a good shot and I had not gathered much information. The Irishman was the first of the last six away and there was everything to play for. When he got to the tee I told him what Lee had hit, but maybe the wind had changed direction slightly so it might be better to go with what he felt. The Irishman is never in a hurry, which is not to say he is slow, but he was definitely not going to rush this shot with his match precariously balanced. I read his mind, and I could tell he was between clubs. Everybody was expectant because it was a crucial shot.

Suddenly he looked round, spotted me and called me over. I got this terrible sinking feeling as I walked across the tee because I knew he wanted to know what club to hit. My only thought was that this could be the first time a captain had ever mis-clubbed a player to lose the Ryder Cup. It was not a nice feeling. I thought, 'My God. I'm going to be responsible for the whole thing right here.' Padraig soon confirmed what I had suspected: he was between a smooth six iron and a big seven. I had no idea what to advise, but finally opted for the suggestion that he would probably be better off with a smooth six because whatever wind there was, it was slightly hurting. I always feel its better to hit a good shot with the wrong club than a bad shot with the right club, so in this case it was whatever he felt happier with.

I retreated back to the bench, holding my breath, and only exhaled when he hit quite a good shot 25 feet left of the pin. It *was* the right club, but it had frightened the hell out of me thinking that I could have blown everything.

Mechanico, unfortunately, ran out of steam against Pate, and Sergio fell victim to Furyk, but Padraig came through. He actually had two putts for the match on the last green and told me afterwards all he could think of as he stood over the first was the point I had been hammering in all week: 'If you've got . . .' He had, and he did.

We really needed Olly to win now. Sergio had joined me by the time his fellow countryman was coming down seventeen. Olly had already been put off his shot to the green by a nasty piece of abuse from the gallery. He looked in the direction of the shout and definitely was not happy. Eventually, Olly and Leonard reached the green. I was halfway down when Leonard putted. It was just one putt, but it sparked the most disgraceful scenes ever seen at a golfing event.

The ball travelled 45 feet to the hole and dropped. Almost before it disappeared every man and woman within range ran on or round the green to congratulate Leonard. There were people on the green. They thought it was all over. It was not, but that did not stop the celebrations. They were all oblivious to the fact that Olly still had a putt to halve the hole and send the match down the last all square. The Americans, players and crowd alike, thought that was it.

I could not believe what I was seeing, and neither could Sergio. He sprinted off towards the green, but there was nothing anybody could do apart from wait for everything to die down. Monty was playing behind Olly and Leonard, and could only shake his head in amazement at what was happening ahead. 'I felt sure when the celebrations finished that they would all walk on to the next tee, but then I saw Olly standing there on his own trying to make a putt and I thought it was unbelievable.'

The scene was ridiculous, but, amazingly, it was not the first time it had happened. In the 1996 President's Cup, Fred Couples holed a 40-footer right at the end of a match against Vijay Singh and every man and his dog ran across Vijay's line to get to Couples. The International team were livid and called US Tour commissioner Tim Finchem into their team room to discuss the matter. The Americans had obviously not learnt an awful lot from that incident.

Here, we had Tom Lehman trying to break the 100 metres record in an effort to get to Leonard, and he acted as the Pied Piper for many more. No respect for Olly, the match or the game was shown. Soon after Lehman ran on to the green, Sky presenter Andrew Castle, who did a great job with his cameraman Brian Bladgett trying to interview at crucial moments, pushed a microphone towards Sam Torrance and asked him what he made of it. Sam was suitably scathing. 'Calls himself a man of God? That was the most disgraceful thing I have ever seen.' It was a soundbite used all over the world. I thought it not so much a question of Lehman's beliefs, more an indication of moral downfall. He has always regarded himself as somebody who upheld the values of the game and its etiquette, but on this day he was way off the mark to the extent that I will never be able to look on him in the same light again.

At least Lehman was consistent in his view on the situation, although he has always seemed to stop short of apologising. 'It was over-exuberance, no question about it, and it was not a good thing,' he was quoted as saying. 'Sometimes you get carried away, but the Europeans celebrated a lot at Valderrama. Today it was their turn to watch.' We watched all right, and we listened, and what we saw and heard did not belong on a golf course.

After witnessing the entire scene, Sir Michael Bonallack, until 1999 the secretary of the Royal & Ancient, summed up the situation with typical candour. 'I felt embarrassed for golf,' he said. 'It went way beyond the decency you associate with proper golf. I love the Ryder Cup, but I do not want to see it degenerate into a mob demonstration every time we play it.'

I got up to the green pretty much as the mayhem was subsiding, and Olly prepared to take his putt. Not surprisingly, considering how long he had had to wait and the indentations on his line, he missed. Only at that point did the USA win the match. Ben Crenshaw bent down and kissed the grass, which was not out of character with his behaviour on the last day, although, if he makes a habit of it, one day he is going to catch a nasty disease. He had been quite theatrical, pumping up the crowd along with some of his players, and had been quite successful at it.

I suppose I was semi-stunned, and I was not really sure where to go or what to do. I had never previously experienced anything like it. I could cope with the disappointment of defeat, having had plenty of practice at it, but to be so closely involved in something which was so alien to my sport, so degrading and intolerable, left me drained and empty inside.

Paul Lawrie had already won by this stage, and the last match left on course was the one we thought might be pivotal to the entire day. Unfortunately that was not the case as Monty came down the last with Stewart. The people of America should be ashamed at some of the things shouted at Monty. I know Payne was, because on several occasions he apologised to him, telling Monty that if there was anything he could do, he would. He was a true gentleman, steeped in the traditions on which some of his fellow countrymen were trampling. It was just a pity his spirit of sportsmanship and sense of fair play did not rub off on to all his colleagues.

Their match eventually meant nothing to the overall result, only to the actual figures attached to victory and defeat. Everybody seemed to think that Payne had conceded the hole, but that was not, initially at least, the case. Having been in a bunker, he had got to within fifteen feet in three, while Monty had been just outside him in two. Payne had said, 'Shall we call it a half?' but, quite rightly, Monty had replied, 'I'll putt.' He had been done out of half a point by Seve at Valderrama when a putt Scott Hoch was hardly likely to have made on the last hole was conceded once European victory was secured. Monty was not going to have that happen again, and Payne thought it was all a bit futile, so then, and only then, had the match been conceded.

Payne and several of the other American players, especially those in the second half of the draw, were not guilty of any form of incitement, but some in the top half behaved very oddly, to say the least. Their conduct was a blight on what had been a golf competition of a very high quality.

Day 3 Singles

Match 17: Lee Westwood v. Tom Lehman

It was a match which started under strange and disturbing circumstances on the first tee, Lehman raising Lee's eyebrows as he conducted the crowd in song. It was an obvious attempt to whip up the home gallery into some kind of frenzy. Lee is level-headed enough to cope with such incidents, though, and showed how much he was in control of his nervous system by holing a testing five-footer on the first, an act Lehman duplicated. Putts of that length are never welcome so early in the round and can prove real heart-stoppers.

Although Lee missed the green on the short second and Lehman found the putting surface, it was the Englishman who would finish closer in two after a delightful chip. The half was the second of three, but the fourth hole broke the stalemate. The American took the lead for the first time with a six-foot birdie putt after Lee missed from twice the distance. The initiative would never be lost.

It quickly became two up when Lehman, not for the first or last time, holed a putt which was much easier to miss, this time from fifteen feet. Lee knew he had to keep pressing, even though he could afford no mistakes, and it looked like his persistence would pay off on the sixth when he rolled in his first birdie, but Lehman matched it. Lehman then hit close to the short seventh, but Lee went closer, and a ten-foot birdie putt gave him his first win. Another chance came to square the match at the next, but the ball refused to drop, although it was agonisingly close.

Lee never surrendered, but there was a growing feeling that this would not be his day. A missed three-foot putt on the ninth restored Lehman's two-hole lead. When Lee failed from ten feet on the tenth, he had made back-to-back bogeys, was three down and was not looking too happy. 'I threw two holes away and I could not afford to do that when Tom was playing as well as he was,' he said later.

Lehman, playing flawless golf, continued to put the pressure on Lee, who nevertheless holed a testing putt to stay three down after eleven holes. But the par four thirteenth would prove the crucial win for the American when he went four up thanks to an eighteen-foot birdie putt from the fringe.

Lehman proceeded to high-five and sprint his way to the fourteenth hole, with the match still alive. Not for the first or last time that day it was conduct unbecoming a professional golfer. Lehman tried to explain his behaviour later, when he said, 'I was really excited about that one, but that's what the Ryder Cup brings out in you. People that are normally laid back and placid can get really emotional.'

But he was playing well. Whenever he had the putter in his hands it seemed he would only need to use it once. The only question seemed to be where the match would end, not whose favour it would be in. Lee was coughing against thunder, and eventually had to shake hands on the sixteenth green. The USA had the start they prayed for and we hoped to avoid.

USA win 3 & 2

Match 18: Darren Clarke v. Hal Sutton

Darren had been positive all week, and when the Ulsterman is in that zone he is capable of shooting low, but he was up against the USA's top points scorer from the first two days and another player capable of putting a rash of birdies on his card.

We needed something from at least one of the top two matches, and the omens looked good when, after missing the green with his approach, Clarke chipped in for an opening birdie and a win. Our joy, like much of what happened throughout the day, was short-lived: three holes later, Sutton had not only gone ahead, but by two shots, holing from twenty feet for a birdie on the second, benefiting from a missed three-footer by Darren on the third, and finding a four good enough to claim the next.

Sutton also enjoyed pumping his fists in celebration, and the crowd responded. If the American was 'working the gallery', he was being paid overtime. He was definitely on the borderline of what can be termed 'acceptable behaviour' on a golf course, and in my opinion he stepped over the line. 'We knew we had to set the pace and get the crowd involved,' he said afterwards. 'The crowd was incredible, and you could feel it on every shot. You could hear the roars all over the course, so you had an idea things were going pretty well.' It was not sweet music to our ears.

Sutton's momentum was arrested on the fifth, but it was only a temporary halt as he claimed the sixth when his approach finished dead. What luck there was going in this match was moving the USA's way, and it was another case of when not if as the American went four up on the twelfth with a par. Darren dug in, but eventually he ran out of holes, and there were still two left to play when Sutton closed it out.

Although the match was only the second off and we had started the day four points ahead, Sutton's point had brought the match level because there was even more prolific scoring in the two matches that followed, and both had finished before the handshake in this one.

USA win 4 & 2

Match 19: Jarmo Sandelin v. Phil Mickelson

If there was ever likely to be a flashpoint – and the chances of that were considerable in this cauldron of a Ryder Cup Sunday – then this match was the favourite to provide it. The American said he had been expecting gamesmanship from his opponent, but afterwards praised Jarmo for his gentlemanly behaviour. I had expected nothing less of him, and every member of my team behaved the same way. Why the Americans should have been worried about our behaviour I have no idea.

Jarmo was the first of the three making their debuts to see action, and he looked nerveless when opening with a solid four and drilling his tee shot at the second to no more than two and a half feet. Mickelson missed from twelve feet to give the Swede his first chance of success. Unfortunately, although close to the hole, he was above it and would have had more chance holing from a much further distance below the cup. At least he hit it, but the ball spun out.

Brookline holds no real terrors for players of this class as long as they stay in play off the tee, but Jarmo paid the price for straying into the rough on the third and lost to a par. He then hit to twelve feet on the fourth, only for Mickelson to finish half as far away. The resulting birdie took him two up, an advantage he held on to after holing from eight feet on the next. The Americans were definitely putting the eyes out of the ball.

An immaculate chip by Jarmo to the sixth won him some applause, and the hole. Now it was Mickelson's turn to come under pressure, but a double bogey on the tenth handed the American his two-hole lead back, and another match began to turn ugly for us. There was no way back from this, and long before it had finished yet another head-to-head looked to be moving towards a damage limitation exercise.

Mickelson revealed afterwards that the Americans had had a very interesting team meeting the previous evening when they had talked about what the late Harvey Penick, highly respected coach to Ben Crenshaw, among others, would have said. The conclusion was: 'Take dead aim.' They were certainly doing that. And Governor George W. Bush had addressed them using a quote from somebody who had stood at the Alamo (the battle, not the rent-a-car desk). The man was helping to hold off 2,000 troops, the odds were stacked up against the defenders, but he was going to fight to the end. Quite what killing people and golf have in common escapes me, but that is America for you.

But Mickelson was spot on in one thing he said. 'Jarmo showed nothing but class and sportsmanship today. I want to commend him.'

USA win 4 & 3

Match 20: Jean Van de Velde v. Davis Love III

When Jean joined the action he became the first Frenchman to play in the Ryder Cup, but Love quickly turned it into a baptism of fire. A first-hole bogey after Jean drove into a bunker gave the USA the initiative, but the early error was rectified by a thirty-foot birdie putt on the third to square the match. When Jean's putting is at its best, there are few who can live with him, and I was hoping this would be one of his hottest days. Love's game, unfortunately, was hotter.

Love was one of those I was convinced Brookline had been tailored for, because he can launch the ball prodigious distances, as he proceeded to demonstrate. Jean had the chance to sneak ahead on the fourth, but his six-footer for the hole slipped by on the right. Love's chip from the top of a bunker on the fifth was the shot that proved pivotal to the match. It found the hole, whereas Jean's attempt hit the pin and stayed out.

Not even a birdie was good enough to win the sixth, then Jean paid the ultimate penalty for missing a four-footer on the seventh. Back-to-back birdies on the tenth and eleventh put Love four up, and once again we were looking at a situation where there would be no way back. Jean followed Love's birdie spree with successive bogeys, and the match was over with five holes unplayed.

It was a great shame the Frenchman did not have more of an opportunity to show the American nation what a good player he is, but that was the way things went and, given the circumstances again, I would have done exactly the same.

USA win 6 & 5

Match 21: Andrew Coltart v. Tiger Woods

If anybody on his Ryder Cup debut was likely to be unfazed at having to face the world number one, it was Andrew Coltart. Like Paul Lawrie, he has the ability to play his own game whatever the scenario and pressure, and so it proved. A variety of circumstances, most outside his control, would conspire against him, but there would be honour in defeat. The Scot played some extremely good golf, did not enjoy the best of fortune, and certainly suffered at the hands, or feet, of the gallery.

World ranking certainly counted for nothing in the first few holes and Andrew was unlucky not to be ahead as he surprised the American galleries, if not us, with his tenacity and ability. When the deadlock was broken it was by Woods, however, but only after Andrew's putt for a half peered over the hole and refused to drop. The American made the most of his fortune, and emphasised it on the next. If the Scot was unfortunate to be down at all, it was cruel that he should be two back after eight, but Woods does have a habit of hitting amazing shots when he needs them most. With Andrew fifteen feet away in two on the par four eighth, Woods missed the green and did not have a promising lie, but downtown Boston heard the roars when he chipped in, the ball disappearing when there was still plenty of speed on it. 'I was just hoping I would get up and down,' Woods said. On such things are matches turned.

There was so little likelihood of Andrew losing an errant tee shot on the next that he never even reloaded, but the search for the ball not only took him over the five-minute maximum, but was also conducted, at the crowd's insistence, a long way from where the ball was eventually found. As a result, from a position where Andrew should, at worst, have been one down, he found himself three down, and chasing the match.

Andrew never gave up that chase but, as for colleagues ahead of him, holes would run out, and it ended on the sixteenth when Woods holed from three feet. Andrew, typically, offered no excuses. 'It was always going to be tough to play any of the Americans today because they were so far behind they had to go for everything.'

USA win 3 & 2

Match 22: Jesper Parnevik v. David Duval

The USA had come out of the blocks without any false starts. Duval, the world number two, who had secured just half a point from the three available in his previous matches and had been subjected to some unnecessary comments from American supporters, would prove no different. Indeed, he was the fastest, and after just six holes was four up. Jesper, who had played as well as anybody on the first two days, had been slightly unsure about whether he wanted to play all five series, and when he needed to be at his best he came up just short.

Duval, like most of his colleagues in the top half of the draw, was so pumped up it seemed he could lay himself open to a suspicion that he, like his extrovert opponent, came from a different planet. The golf he played certainly was not of the type he had produced in either foursomes or fourball. Then again, he had only just started to appreciate just what the Ryder Cup is all about. Referring to it as an 'exhibition match' had not endeared him to certain sections of the galleries, but Boston would change his thinking. His reference point had been two President's Cup matches, in which the USA face the Rest of the World bar Europe, but after this match he would say, 'No offence to the President's Cup, but it pales in comparison.'

There were so many birdies falling it looked like Duval might need a gun dog at one stage. At six down after eight, Jesper needed a miracle. Standing on the thirteenth tee he was dormie six, and he eventually succumbed on the fourteenth green.

It was then that Duval seemed to lose the plot, becoming so animated that I was not sure whether he was going to be carried off by the crowd or by men in white coats. 'I got caught up in the moment,' he said afterwards.

USA win 5 & 4

Match 23: *Padraig Harrington v Mark O'Meara*

O'Meara had made just one start in the previous two days, which was an indication of the form he had shown coming into the matches. He was not at the top of his game, but such a good putter that anything could happen if he started to see the ball drop. The one thing I was certain of was that Padraig would not feel at all inferior when faced with somebody who had won both the US Masters and Open crowns within the last eighteen months.

Padraig had arrived in Boston on a crest, and he was still riding it come Sunday. The fact that O'Meara took him to the eighteenth was testimony to the standard of play at this level. Even when they are generally below their best, the Ryder Cup causes players to search inside for that extra something. 'I tried not to think about who I was playing,' Padraig said. 'But I knew he had been in this kind of situation before, had handled pressure like this and was not going to go away.'

Given what was happening ahead of him, Padraig did not need advising on our critical position and he dug every bit as deep as, and then deeper than, O'Meara. It was quite a time before any hole was halved: Padraig claimed the first, O'Meara the next two, and then the Irishman levelled on the fourth before taking the lead for the second time in the match at the next. Another win looked likely on the sixth, but the ball lipped out.

Next blood went to O'Meara on the eighth with a birdie, but Padraig went ahead for a third time when the American came out of trees to concede the hole. Although two of the world's best putters, neither was having much joy from close range, and after thirteen holes it was back to all square.

Both players had chances to regain the initiative, but they went to the last hole. Padraig played it majestically

– a drive and a wedge from 142 yards to ten feet ('probably the best shot I hit all week', as he later described it). O'Meara found two bunkers, and could not get up and down from the second. Padraig found himself with two putts for the match . . . and he knew what to do with them. A win at last, at the seventh attempt.

Europe win 1 up

Match 24: Miguel Angel Jiménez v. Steve Pate

Mechanico had been one of the players who had amazed Americans with the quality of his play, his shot-making and his composure. It may have been his first Ryder Cup but he had been around for a long time, and his game had matured significantly with age.

I have always had the utmost respect for Pate's game because he always seems to get the best out of it, particularly when he needs to. Here was a case in point, because everybody knew this would be a tough match. What we did not realise was that it would prove to be as crucial as it was.

One went close, then the other. Pate struck on the fourth, Miguel on the sixth. It was nip and tuck all the way and the tension built, although neither player gave any impression that he would be beaten by pressure. A perfect example of this came on the par three seventh when Miguel looked odds-on to win when his ball finished three feet away, while Pate's rolled against a collar at the side of the green. It was not an easy shot, but Pate pulled out a fairway wood, a shot made famous by Tiger Woods, and propelled the ball into the hole.

During this match Pate owned the heavier artillery. A wise choice by captain Crenshaw but one not favoured by Fred Couples' supporters, he was never in total control, but after winning the eighth he took a lead he would never relinquish.

If the match had a defining moment it was on the eleventh green where Mechanico had an eight-footer for birdie and Pate was a foot closer for par. The Spaniard missed, the American did not, and another hole which had looked as if it was going our way went the other.

I had emphasised the need to stick with an opponent, and my words had not been lost on the Spaniard.

If he was going down, he would go down fighting, but needing to win the last two holes to halve the match was too much for him.

USA win 2 & 1

Match 25: José Maria Olazábal v. Justin Leonard

Long before this match was over it was apparent that we would have to win it, and for much of the match it looked odds-on that we would. Olly always seems to find something extra for the Ryder Cup, and he had it in abundance to the turn and the start of the back nine, building a four-hole lead. The thing about Leonard, however, is that he is not one of the world's best putters for nothing. No matter how ordinary his general play is on any particular day, if his putter catches fire, the entire Boston Fire Department does not have the capacity to put it out.

And Leonard's putter was spitting flames. He soon started nibbling into Olly's lead, then bit great chunks out of it, until eventually it disappeared completely. If this comeback started anywhere, it was on the eleventh when a bogey was good enough to secure a half. Had he gone five down, it would have been over. Olly, having looked invincible, started to look vulnerable, and he had to pay the penalty for bogeys on both twelve and thirteen. The fourteenth looked to be heading for a half until Leonard rifled in a birdie.

One hole was all that separated them now, and the momentum had definitely changed sides, Leonard highlighting the fact with a birdie putt a long way across the fifteenth to square the match. There was everything to play for now: if Leonard avoided defeat, the Ryder Cup would be changing hands.

Both reached the seventeenth green in two and Leonard had the longer putt, at about forty feet some ten feet longer than Olly's. It looked like the match would go down the last all square, but Leonard unbelievably sank his putt, and all hell broke loose. The Americans were celebrating because they thought that was it, but Olly still had a putt for the half. He had to wait a long time before he could take it, and when finally he was allowed to address his ball, he missed the hole.

It was cold comfort for Olly that he managed to birdie the last hole to claim a half.

Match halved

Match 26: Colin Montgomerie v. Payne Stewart

This was the second match in succession where a substantial lead was whittled away, but this one had a different ending. It was also the match we had identified as the one most likely to have the deciding influence on the entire outcome. Although Monty won, things did not go entirely to plan.

It was an inauspicious start by both players. The match only came to life when Monty, attracting the worst verbal assaults ever delivered on a golf course, holed a long putt on the fifth to edge ahead. Another birdie on the sixth, followed by a Stewart bogey, meant the Scot held a three-hole advantage, but that was back to one at the turn as Stewart holed from twenty-five feet on the eighth, and then Monty failed to convert from four feet on the ninth.

Both players had chances after that, before Monty went back to two up on the twelfth with a twelve-footer for par. But Stewart hung in there, and wins on both fourteen and fifteen meant it was all square with three to play.

They were still that way on the eighteenth green. Monty had got there in two, while Stewart was fifteen feet away in three. The match was over. Stewart offered Monty a half, but Monty said he would putt, and only then was the hole conceded. It was the last action of the 33rd Ryder Cup.

Europe win 1 up

Match 27: Sergio Garcia v. Jim Furyk

Sergio had been a revelation in the team room and on the course in his first Ryder Cup. He was unbeaten through four matches going into his singles match, and he was hoping that this would be the one which decided the Ryder Cup in our favour, but Furyk proved too good for him on the day. As Sergio thought, there was indeed every chance this could prove one of the pivotal matches, so I made sure the teenager was not lacking for support, although he did admit afterwards that he had found it different playing on his own after four matches with a partner.

Early sparring brought wins for both, and after seven holes it was all square. Furyk may not have the most graceful swing in golf, but it is definitely effective, and gradually he started to get one of the game's most dangerous putting strokes in top gear and slowly pushed the match out of the Spaniard's reach.

It started with an eighteen-footer on the eighth, and Furyk went two clear as Sergio failed to get up and down from a bunker on the eleventh. Not too bad yet, but the difference stretched to three on the twelfth when Furyk this time found the bottom of the cup from twenty feet. Another win then left Furyk in a position on the fifteenth tee from which it was impossible to lose, and he closed the match on that green.

Furyk's win meant that the USA needed just half a point to reclaim the Ryder Cup.

USA win 4 & 3

Match 28: Paul Lawrie v. Jeff Maggert

The Open champion had been one of our many successes on the first two days and had announced himself as a player on the world stage. He would enhance his reputation here, but alas, it was too little too late.

After going one up at the second thanks to a superb tee shot to three feet, Paul would never again be out of the lead. The fourth proved fruitful when he holed from fourteen feet, and after his approach to the eighth landed in the shadow of the flag he was three ahead.

The biggest blow to Maggert's hopes came on the par five ninth when he finished in the short rough to the left of the green, while Paul was in deeper stuff over the back. Both chipped to no further away than three feet, but while Paul found the cup, Maggert could not, and entering the back nine the American was four back and on the way to defeat.

Maggert did not have the game this day to get back at Paul, and he finally succumbed on the fifteenth green. 'Paul never really let me in the match,' he said later.

Europe win 4 & 3

USA 14 ½ EUROPE 13 ½

I was genuinely upset when it was all over, but I found Ben and said, 'Well done.' And I meant it, because I was pleased for him. He had done a lot of hard work and been faced with quite a few delicate problems. I was simply cross about some of the things that had happened on the course, and even more so afterwards. I have never minded losing as a professional golfer because it is something you face most of the time – when you are as bad as me, almost all the time. That was not a problem, but I like the game to be held in some esteem, and it was not that day.

After shaking hands with Ben, I went back to the locker room with all the others and sat down for a few minutes to recover. Straight after something like that, the players just want to be with one another. It was not a happy place, and a number of us were very upset; quite a few towels were handed round, and as many heads thrust into them. A lot had been put into the week, we had tasted victory almost at one stage, and to come up just short was very hard to take. I did not say anything because I was incapable of speech. I cried openly and unashamedly. It had been bottled up inside for a long time, and it just came out. You never know who is going to be affected most. Sam normally cries at the drop of a hat, but he was in control here, along with one or two others. Quite often, those guys who show less emotion on the course can crack up completely afterwards, but there was no hiding anybody's disappointment here.

It had only ever happened to me once before, after we lost in 1993. The pressure is considerable, and when it is all over the emotions of it all can be uncontrollable. Now, as then, I just let it out of my system. There was nothing we could change about the result now, although I already felt there would be something we could do eventually to prevent the way it had panned out from happening again. I think how I reacted surprised some of the boys because I had tried to be in control and at least make them think I knew what I was doing all week. For them to see me so upset was very different, but within fifteen minutes it was all under control and we were ready to go out and thank our supporters.

After seeking solace in a couple of Budweisers, our emotions were in check, we had accepted the defeat and admitted America had played some magnificent golf to beat us. There would be no squabbling about the result, just the manner of it. The 400-yard walk to the closing ceremony was the longest of my life, but it had to be done and this time I was less apprehensive about what I was going to say and who I was going to thank. I knew exactly who would not get a mention.

I thanked my entire team, and particularly the three guys who had not played for two days. Their attitude, enthusiasm and commitment had been nothing short of magnificent and my words were not said lightly. They had had to make a sacrifice in the interests of what I thought was best for the team, and I appreciated it. As it turned out we lost, so anybody can argue that I did not do the right thing, but all I know is that in the same position, under identical circumstances, as I have said, I would do exactly the same again. Andrew, Jarmo and Jean had been a great help, as had my assistants, Ken and Sam, whom I thanked from the podium along with the wives, and particularly my own. Jane had done a wonderful job getting through mountains of work and a fair bit of hassle. I thanked the caddies too, whose work is not always as appreciated as it should be, and that seemed to please them: they jumped up and down in the distance, their normal rowdy selves, looking as if nobody had ever spoken to them before. I then thanked my immediate predecessors, Seve Ballesteros and Bernard Gallacher, the PGA of America, the European Ryder Cup Committee and the Brookline Country Club, and congratulated Ben and Julie. Finally, I thanked the European supporters, but I was careful not to offer similar sentiments to the American spectators. I did not feel their behaviour had warranted it.

I was slightly subdued at the final, official press conference, although Jarmo made up for everybody who was not feeling in the best of moods. 'I love you all,' he said. 'Thank you. I love you there, I love you here, I love you everywhere. That has been our key – team spirit.' Good old Jarmo.

My initial thoughts were for my magnificent team. 'It's been an honour to lead them,' I said. 'They have given me more than 100 per cent and we came up just short. Nothing was left to chance, and we gave it our best shot. All the guys showed such commitment and enthusiasm. It was nothing short of fantastic. The spirit in the side was remarkable, and this team was definitely a case of the whole being greater than the sum of the parts.'

The first question was predictably about events on the seventeenth green, and Olly dealt with it graciously. 'That kind of behaviour is not the one anybody expects, especially when you are playing in a match and the entire result might rest on it,' he said. 'It was very sad to see, an ugly picture, but you must be the judges of it. If you did not see it there then watch it on television and make up your own minds.' Olly was then pushed into talking about a role reversal, how we might have reacted under similar circumstances. 'We would have shown emotion, but we would have behaved like we should,' he replied. 'That is what happened at Valderrama when the matches were very close. The thing is what happened today should not have happened. We are playing a match and we should show respect to each other and what happened was not the right thing to do. I understand there was a lot of emotion, but at the same time you have to have your feet on the ground and realise what the situation is. I understand that you are carried by emotion and sometimes you do things you would not normally. There is nothing wrong in that, but you should show respect for your opponent. As long as you do that then you can cheer your team as much as you want.'

I agreed totally with Olly, and a spontaneous outbreak of applause from the team suggested they were feeling the same way. As I looked along the line I knew my players would not have behaved like that had they won, although I did not blame Ben Crenshaw for his or the crowd's reaction. The suggestion that Ben may have outmanoeuvred me did not fit comfortably with my reading of the day's events, and the speed with which I replied may have suggested I was not altogether in agreement. 'I think we were outplayed,' I admitted. 'I think the way they played and the shots and putts flowing into the hole from all angles, tactics would not have made much difference. It got to the stage where I knew they must stop holing them and we must start, but they just went and holed a lot more. It was quite remarkable, but that is what you have to do in this game, ride the streak, and they rode tremendously well today which is why we came up just a little short.

Jesper expanded on the theme. 'You could feel the momentum definitely building,' he said. 'They pretty much ran us over, and as soon as they got the first six matches so easily, the crowd was bound to get involved, as were the other players.'

He had a point. The only thing that might have stopped the American momentum was a bomb scare. My team had held the initiative on Saturday afternoon, but gradually it changed. Unfortunately, nothing similar happened 24 hours later, and we were powerless to do anything about it.

Monty was as gracious in defeat as he had been whenever fate had not been kind to him on a golf course. 'The Americans played very well today, but we did really well considering we came here as massive underdogs. What we did for the first two days was unbelievable, and we should take great heart in what we achieved because we gave the USA a big fright.' When Monty failed to rise to the bait of another loaded question about crowd behaviour, Jesper said what we all felt. 'It should not ever happen. I am kind of a little American on the European team because I live over here, and I had a lot of friends in the gallery today and they were embarrassed just to hear some of the heckling that happened to Monty, for example. I know you all laugh when he says he uses it as a motivation factor, but it should not happen. I can understand the Americans rooting for their own, but it should never get personal in golf.' Paul Lawrie, Monty's partner for two days, echoed that view. 'Some of the things that were said to him were just disgusting,' he said. 'The people who shout out these ridiculous things should not be allowed to go to golf tournaments.'

When the questioning reverted to the less controversial although still contentious issue of sitting out three players for two days, I pointed out that the decisions we had taken had been done so as a team. I felt they had been the right decisions and that we would do the same again. If someone had said to us at the start of the week, 'Those three guys don't play for two days, you play those nine four times, but you've got a four-point lead going into the singles,' we would have gone to the swimming pool for two days and come out on Sunday.

Given the events of the afternoon, it was fitting that Olly should have the last word. He was speaking for us all when he said, 'I think we all want to congratulate the American team. We are not trying to find any excuse from talking about the behaviour on seventeen or anywhere else. We congratulate them, and next time it will be for the benefit of the game of golf if we manage to behave just a little bit better, every one of us. Thank you very much.'

After that we returned to the team room at the course, where the caddies were going bananas – singing, dancing and generally being caddies. It did not take long to wash the smell of defeat from our hands, and it was nice just to be able to sit down, wind down and sink a few drinks. The mood lightened considerably during that hour. Nothing more could go wrong, thank heavens. It just shows how wrong you can be.

Just when we thought nothing could happen to make matters worse, it did, as we made our move to leave the course for the last time to return to the hotel. Nobody could believe their eyes when we got to the locker room and found it had been completely rifled. Absolutely everything had been taken: shoes, umbrellas, hats, waterproofs, signed pictures, personal belongings, and everything we had been collecting to give away to charity. The thieves, whoever they were, left nothing. We had lost, the game had publicly been robbed of its integrity, and now we had been cleaned out. Welcome to the USA. Have a nice day.

Just when that sinking feeling had been lifted, down we went again, but nothing would stop us from having a good old knees-up back at the hotel. Even that would not be without its drama.

David Feherty, one of our former Ryder Cup and tour colleagues, now making a huge name for himself on American television, had popped into the team room at the course to commiserate, as had Christy O'Connor Jr, the Belfry hero of 1989. Pros never mind fellow pros joining the party – they are usually more than welcome – so I invited them to join us for a drink in the players' room at the hotel. A few of the boys, including Monty, had gone back earlier and were unaware of my invitation. Unknown to me at the time, I had innocently made a big mistake in asking Feherts, a friend of mine over many years, to join us. His presence would be something Monty could not cope with.

At the hotel I had a quick soak and a few more drinks, and then Jane, who had been in the team room earlier, came back to tell me Monty was not happy. He was angry that David Feherty was there, and wanted him thrown out. It had all been sorted out before I got there, but I went to find out what had happened because I did not realise there was a history between the two.

Apparently, Monty had made it clear as soon as he saw his Kiawah Island colleague that his presence was not welcome. The reason was that a few years earlier, when Feherts started commentating in the States, he had been the one who had told his audience – several million strong – that Monty's nickname over in Europe was Mrs Doubtfire. It was a sobriquet very, very few people had known about because it does not exactly slip off the tongue. But Americans latched on to it quickly, and the nickname had not only become widely known, but was used against Monty by hecklers. Monty never forgave Feherts for that.

When it was pointed out, Feherts made a hasty exit and went to the public bar downstairs. I had no idea about the situation between the two of them; had I known it would be a problem I would not have asked him back. Feherts is a good friend I get on well with, but I certainly did not want to compromise the position of the team. Their needs and feelings came first for the whole week, and Sunday night was no exception. I wanted the players to at least have a fairly relaxed evening, drink whatever they wanted and get over what had happened. It had been a tough day, but you have to move on, and I wanted everybody to be able to deal with things in their own way. Certainly, once I found out the reason behind Monty's request I was entirely behind the Scotsman. Some things do not bear repeating to the public, and what Feherts had broadcast was something which was to haunt Monty over the next few years.

Monty was calmed by David's departure, and the rest of the evening was spent having a few laughs and quite a few more beers. Quite a few of the caddies came back, and it is always good to see them on a Sunday night because they are part of the team. They joined us and told a few stories, having a good chuckle and generally forgetting what had happened on the golf course that day.

Prince Andrew popped in briefly, but long enough for Darren's caddie, Billy Foster, as Yorkshire as Ilkley Moor, to invite him to his home course, Bingley St Ives, to partner him in the club's Open day. Billy told Prince Andrew he would give him a good night down at the pub and assured him he would enjoy the course. 'There'll be no hassle,' said Billy. 'Just give me your number and I'll ring you.' I think Billy received a very diplomatic and royal reply.

The tour's chief executive, Ken Schofield, also came to say well done, and his words were, as ever, much appreciated. If a non-player comes into the team room they have to be fairly close to somebody otherwise the atmosphere can change very quickly. In that situation it is best to leave the players to themselves, but Ken was always welcome. He has done so much for our tour, and I do not think anybody could feel more passionately about the success or failure of it. He lives and breathes every tournament, and he is always looking for alternative ways to develop, expand and improve. The players appreciate what he and his deputy, George O'Grady – two very different people who fit well together – have done and are always happy to welcome them into their normally private domain.

It was strange that none of the Americans came down from the floor above to join us, as they had done after previous Ryder Cups, win, lose or draw. Perhaps they were embarrassed. Some should have been. Right up until we left to board Concorde we saw none of them, although in my experience they still tended to go to bed fairly early, even after winning.

There was also a serious edge to our evening, because the more we talked afterwards the more information about what had gone on surfaced. A grim canvas of controversy was developing. It seemed the players had been repeatedly put off by shouts from the crowd. A ridiculous amount of heckling, shouting and general nastiness had sullied the cleanest of sports.

Andrew Mair, a friend and partner in a golf design business, told us he had been astounded to find when he arrived at the course that people were being allowed in without tickets. He decided to test things out and went back out again, returning with the general throng and not once being stopped. Without proper ticket checking, no wonder there seemed to be a big crowd there. They were just letting anybody in, regardless of whether or not they had credentials. Some of our drivers told us that although they were there for the full seven days they were only working for a total of twelve hours. I know they are all volunteers, but that seemed a short working week. It seemed that the method of increasing the crowd was not to check tickets and to get a load of volunteers on very short hours.

Sitting in the stand behind the eighteenth, Andrew heard somebody sitting close by ask a friend who exactly was on his way up the fairway. 'It's Monty,' somebody replied, to which came the retort, 'All right, we won't let him putt.' There were many instances of that kind of attitude. It has to be said that the vast majority of people there were good fun and friendly, but the minority causing problems this time was bigger than ever before. Golf was not 'the winner'.

Our minds were slightly less focused on the horrors of the day when we retired, at about 2.30 a.m., for a couple of hours' sleep before an early start for the airport. But it had been one helluva day.

11 Home James

I T WAS ABOUT 9 A.M. WHEN WE LEFT the Four Seasons for the last time, but not before we had said our goodbyes and thank yous to the manager, Robin. Nobody could have looked after us better, and our stay downtown at what was a fantastic hotel where we wanted for nothing was definitely high on the list of pluses for the week.

I thought Ben might come to see us off, but maybe it is not the done thing in the USA, so we headed straight for the airport, through the roadworks, to find the autograph hunters and the press waiting. We had built up a full picture by this time of the previous day's events, and it was not a pretty one. I was more than willing to give my point of view, for the game of golf had been tainted and I saw no point in hiding the fact.

By the time our fairly subdued group boarded Concorde, we had started to talk about the big picture. Overall, we felt we had done a good job. We had given it our best shot and had performed well. We had lost, by the narrowest of margins, but had behaved with dignity, unlike some of their players, and definitely their crowd and marshals. We could take some consolation from that fact. We were not celebrating, but neither were we particularly down, and that is how we were as we sped over the Atlantic.

We had all got to know people we never really knew at all before the week started, so the goodbyes at the airport had a little more to them than is normal. We had shared many things and been very close, and there is no doubt you do feel different about other players after a Ryder Cup week, and it is something you carry through your life. In a Ryder Cup situation, you tend to dig a bit deeper.

A few of the guys were off on a private jet to the German Masters, others went their own ways. Jane and I hired a car, picked up my clubs from the Hilton, and headed off up the M1. Ahead of me was at least one week of press bombardment and another few days' winding down before life could return to normal.

It was only when I returned to the peace and comfort of my Yorkshire home that I was able to sit down and fully reflect on what had happened at Brookline. Eight years down the line, the lessons of Kiawah Island in 1991 were forgotten. We had not liked the Desert Storm hats there because they were used as a tool for winding up the crowd. They appeared to have missed the fact that we fought alongside the Americans in the Gulf and that there was a long history of Great Britain and the USA working together. All of a sudden they seemed to want to turn it into a war on the shore. There had been some incidents with the crowd, and people had pledged after the match that it would not be allowed to happen again. Galleries had to be controlled and players respected. We thought then that the Ryder Cup had a big problem. Looking back, it had had a small one.

There is undoubtedly a major concern this time over the Ryder Cup, no matter what the Americans thought. If bad behaviour is allowed to continue, or spill over into regular golf events, then the very nature of the game will be changed, and that will be an extremely sad day. We will be forced to play in conditions where there is constant noise, but it is not meant to be that way.

I received a lot of supportive letters on a similar theme. 'If it means so much to them, then why not let them keep it?' said one. It was understandable that people should think that way because there was definitely some desperation in what went on that Sunday. One of the sad facts was that there was absolutely no need for such behaviour because the American team played some great golf and, taking everything into consideration, probably deserved their win. But we certainly did not deserve to be treated the way we were at the course. In fact, no guest, golfer or Ryder Cup player should have to put up with that sort of behaviour. We were made to feel like intruders.

The press, understandably again, had a field day. But I must say that in Europe I cannot remember reading a single thing I disagreed with, and our journalists are normally the first to have a go at our sportsmen when they lose. Now, as in the build-up to the event and the event itself, the reporting was balanced and accurate. The tabloid headlines captured the full story: 'United Slobs of America' screamed the *Mirror*; the *Express* ran with 'Horror Show'; the *Sun* went with 'Disgusting'; the *Mail* used the word 'Disgraceful'. And there was no stopping some. 'American players and their fans belong in the gutter', it said in the *Sun*, while *Evening Standard* columnist Matthew Norman could not contain himself. 'They are repulsive people,' he wrote. 'Charmless, rude, cocky, mercenary, humourless, ugly, full of nauseatingly fake religiosity and as odious in victory as they are unsporting in defeat.' It was probably a good job he did not try to search for any bad points.

All seemed to make the point that there was winning and there was winning. The USA had won the Ryder Cup, but lost in terms of dignity. 'A fantastic competition was sullied by a football-terrace culture outside the ropes and an appalling lack of consideration from team

America inside them', the *Standard* reported, while the *Mirror* backed its headline with the words: 'Football hooligans act better than the way Americans have treated the Ryder Cup over the last three days. Their antics whipped the crowd into uncontrolled boorish behaviour. Sporting relations between the two nations have slipped to an all-time low.' The *Mail* said that the redneck show had taken the sport to the stage where punches could be exchanged instead of pleasantries.

The tabloids were not alone in their denunciation of the bedlam at Brookline. The *Daily Telegraph* wrote: 'Americans not only indulged in the worst excesses of triumphalism during and after the match, but also turned in a repulsive display of bad manners.' And the flak was not just flying from our side of the Atlantic either. Judging from the many letters I have received and the newspapers and magazines I have read, there was plenty of criticism of American behaviour from within. I quote selectively, but the general tenor of the reporting is similar. *Sports Illustrated*'s David Fleming:

> The US team's behaviour on the seventeenth green after Justin Leonard holed a 45-foot putt was indeed one of the most incredible, monumental and shocking examples of poor sportsmanship and lack of class or composure that I have ever witnessed in golf – or probably any other sport, for that matter . . . Can you imagine what we'd all be saying if putts were reversed and the Europeans celebrated like that before Leonard could hit his shot? Please. We'd probably be at war right now . . . Remember, athletic competition does not build character, it just reveals it. And when it starts getting hard to differentiate between the behaviour at a golf match and a pro-wrestling match, we're all doomed, folks . . . It's not about

America v. Europe. Never was. Hell, it's not even about winning or losing. It's about something more important and even more rare in the world today. Class. Humility. Sportsmanship. And at this moment, our Ryder Cup runneth empty.

But it was not all one-way traffic. Fleming's colleague, Gary Van Sickle, writing for the same organ, awarded my players and the European media his 'biggest crybabies award' for complaining about the spontaneous celebrations on the seventeenth green.

Yes, it was poor form, but everyone simply forgot Olazábal still had a putt to tie, including several Euro writers I was talking to in the media centre at the time, who said 'It's over' after Leonard's putt because they forgot too. Funny, I don't remember reading any stories about poor sportsmanship in 1989 at the Belfry when the Europeans were all dancing over the eighteenth green. The Boston fans' heckling of some Euros was far worse and inexcusable, but when it comes to poor sportsmanship, European Ryder Cup galleries are the undisputed champs. You never read about that because the European media types are too busy cheering and booing right among themselves.

And I always thought our scribes watched events from the bar – and there they were cheering and booing all the time. Are you sure? At least it is comforting to know they were actually out there while that particular writer was apparently hobnobbing in the media centre on a day trip from Mars.

If events in Boston left a bitter taste, then Monty was definitely thinking teetotal in his *Daily Telegraph* column. 'I learnt over the weekend that Michelob beer is to be the official drink at the next Ryder Cup. To me that does not make sense. They should be thinking in terms of orange juice', he wrote. Drink was certainly taken in Boston, and this is one area I feel very strongly about too. Nobody should be allowed to bring alcohol on to the course from outside; it should only be drunk on the course in areas where it is being dispensed.

It did seem that some people at Boston, Ben Crenshaw included, had not fully taken on board the basis of our complaints. It had nothing to do with the fact that we lost. I would have said exactly the same had we won. No doubt Van Sickle would have given us the worst winners award. If his judgement is in doubt, his myopia certainly is not. But Crenshaw was quoted as saying that some of our criticism was born out of frustration. 'When you lose over there and they come out with soccer chants, it stings you,' he said. 'That's what they had this time because we played so convincingly. They knew they were in trouble because those cheers reverberated across the golf course. It's tough to take, but that's what was happening.'

If Crenshaw, who had apologised on the day, was wide of the mark there, he was even wider when he said, 'The Ryder Cup is about partisan support. Believe me, it's no different when we're over there. Just ask some of the players who played at Valderrama. It's not like this has never happened before.' Crenshaw was not at Valderrama. I was, and there was no comparison. Can he tell me how many of the American players were yelled at by spectators while they were hitting shots, or how many of them suffered personal abuse of the worst possible kind? And how many of the American wives in Spain were spat at by the crowd? The answer to all those questions is none. What happened at Brookline broke every record in the book, by a distance.

The more I thought about events and the more I read and listened, the more I was convinced I had to try to do something about it to ensure those terrible sport-degrading scenes would never be repeated. What planet some of the Americans were on I have no idea, but it was nowhere I would ever want to play golf. Jim Awtrey, the executive director of the US PGA, said, 'We had twelve Sergios out there.' That seemed to me a cretinous thing to come out with because Sergio is nineteen, and teenagers do jump up and down. Tiger Woods has been criticised in the past, but I always accepted it because at that age it is rarely premeditated or unpleasant. At that time of their lives, people are exuberant, but the kind of melodrama Tom Lehman and Hal Sutton were going in for at Brookline I find completely unacceptable and totally out of order. It never has and never will have a place in the royal and ancient game.

Lehman wrote me a letter afterwards. It was not one of apology, but explanation, and after reading it I deemed it not much better than a waste of ink. Actually, I have no idea why he wrote it. Then and now, we are poles apart on the subject. He cannot see what was wrong about what happened and believes that things went on at Valderrama which were just as bad. Like Crenshaw, he is wrong about that, and that is simple fact. I was at both, and I was at Kiawah in 1991 when a lot of the Americans held up their hands and said, 'This is not right, now let's get it better.' Brookline was many times worse than Kiawah, yet we have players like Lehman saying, 'What was wrong? I don't understand what you are complaining about.' And then there is Davis Love, who called us 'sore losers', which is just the kind of shallow comment that makes some people feel better. It probably makes them all feel better to think that nothing was wrong. As far as I am concerned, their attitude is just a means of abrogating responsibility.

I was determined to have it out with Lehman, and my chance came at the Dunhill Cup a few weeks after Brookline. He seemed to be keeping a very low profile, and even missed the opening ceremony, but I finally caught up with him on the Friday. He was on the practice ground when I approached him. I said, 'Thanks for the letter, but I don't agree with your explanation of things.' He just said, 'Why are you still going on about it?' Actually, I had not been going on about it. I was merely answering press questions, which is my duty as captain. Our reporters had been stoking the issue, and quite rightly so, and I was happy to lift up the carpet under which some were trying to sweep the Ryder Cup dirt. We had also had a huge amount of support from the American press, as I have said, which I guess a lot of their players had conveniently forgotten about in their quest for self-absolution. I then said to Lehman, 'You said you wanted to forget about the whole thing, but I thought there was a problem which should not be forgotten about, but which should be learnt from and acted upon.' It did not seem that he would ever see my point of view.

Occasionally, it seems Lehman does not see anything wrong with unorthodox behaviour on the course. He was involved in a match on the second afternoon at Brookline, and after holing a putt with Darren Clarke still to play, he started making exaggerated actions with his fist and arm as if he was pulling something. When he finally stopped, Darren knocked in a four-footer and turned round to stare straight at Lehman. They saw each other a few weeks later and Lehman asked Darren if he had been practising his stare, to which he received the reply, 'Why? Have you been practising pulling the toilet chain?'

What really worries me is that if players like Lehman and Love think there is nothing wrong with what happened at Brookline, golf could become like some other sports. What happened to David Duval in Phoenix, when he was heckled and almost pulled out of the tournament, is indicative of that. It is becoming a bit of a disease running through crowds in the USA, and it is time to stop it. The sooner people like Lehman and Love wake up to that fact, the better.

Basically, at St Andrews we did not get anywhere. It was an exchange of views and his opinions were, to me, not consistent with the morals most of us hold dear with regard to the etiquette of golf. It was strange that he should ask me why I was going on about it, because a month afterwards at the WGC at Valderrama he spun one back into the water and a few people cheered, which prompted him to have a real go about that and what happened at the Ryder Cup. I had no idea if things were praying on his mind or whether he was just having a hard time knowing what to say. What I do know is that he has gone down in my estimation.

One player whose behaviour stood out as exemplary at Brookline, as I have said, was Payne Stewart. I did not see him or any of the bottom six do anything of the nature that was happening in the top half of the draw. Payne was also instrumental in trying to get the crowd to quieten down during his match with Monty. He had also been one of the players to say after Kiawah that there was a problem. At Brookline his behaviour was beyond reproach. He showed that you could be a rah-rah, hootin', tootin' flag-waver without crossing the line into boorish behaviour.

I saw Payne on the Tuesday night of Dunhill Cup week in the Jigger, a popular meeting place attached to the Old Course Hotel, where I was having a pre-dinner drink with Jane and the two other English team members, Lee Westwood with his wife Laurae, and David Howell, plus the head of the International Sports Management team Chubby Chandler and his deputy David Brookes. Payne was on his own because his lovely wife Tracey was feeling jet-lagged. Jane asked me to invite Payne over, and he immediately accepted.

To say we gave him hell would be an exaggeration, although he did get it slightly in the neck. But we were not attacking him directly, and anyway, he could handle it. We explained the point of view of all of us who saw what happened on that final day. Payne understood what we were saying. He did not actually admit that some of his fellow players were wrong, but then he had not witnessed most of what happened because he was out there playing Monty. Had he seen it, I know he would have agreed with us because he was very much an upholder of the game's principles. It was a very sad day indeed when he died so tragically soon afterwards. Everybody who knew him, and many who did not, were affected deeply by what happened. The loss to his family was immeasurable, and in the game there is definitely a void. He was popular with his fellow professionals and with the spectators, and that can be quite difficult to achieve.

Payne was definitely one of the good guys, and he thoroughly enjoyed himself that night over dinner. The looks on the faces of a few other diners seemed to suggest they thought it slightly strange that we were eating at the same table, but just because a few people behaved badly does not mean you have to fall out with the entire team. I had no reason to stop liking Payne because he always had a balanced view of things.

After long and careful consideration of the issue, I completed my own balanced assessment of what should happen to ensure the future of the Ryder Cup. My recommendations were:

1. Alcohol should not be brought into the grounds, and should only be consumed in areas where it is served.
2. Incitement of the crowd by players should carry a penalty of loss of hole.
3. The number of people inside the ropes should be restricted, and should be exactly the same number for each team.
4. Strict guidelines for marshals, because those at Brookline were hopelessly inept.
5. Strict security on all gates so that only people with valid tickets are allowed entry.
6. A large number, at least ten, of security guards to follow each match: two inside the ropes to face the crowd, and eight mingling with the galleries so that trouble-makers can be immediately identified and removed.
7. Week-long tickets only to be sold (no separate day passes), so that anybody causing problems has his or her credentials confiscated for the rest of the event.

If my recommendations are accepted I am sure the Ryder Cup will once again take its place as the perfect example of how people should play and respect the game. The last thing I want is for golf to descend into something other sports have become. I do not want fights in the crowds or people to shout obscenities or players not to be able to putt because of the noise. High standards of etiquette and behaviour are things which have distinguished the game throughout the years. Brookline was a big step backwards, and pushed golf into the same hole as some other sports. It should be pulled out and never allowed to sink to that level again. And if we do not come down hard at the next Ryder Cup, it will be too late.

What happened at Brookline has put me off wanting ever again to be involved in a tournament in the USA. It was not only totally unacceptable and unpleasant, but also a huge shame, because in that part of the country the people can be very entertaining, lively and good fun. Take the mickey out of them and they will come straight back with a one-liner that will put you right in your place. That is all part of the fun. Unfortunately, the unruly element was way out of line. I will be trying very hard to make the next Ryder Cup team at the Belfry, but after that, who knows? Maybe I will be daft enough, at the age of 49, to have another go for Detroit.

The Ryder Cup Committee have decided to appoint Sam Torrance as captain for the 2001 Ryder Cup, and I think they are absolutely right. When we were deliberating about who would lead the team at Brookline we eventually decided that whoever did it there, the other would take up the reins in the next one at the Belfry. There is a kind of symmetry involved because it was at the Midlands course where Sam was the hero of the historic triumph in 1985, and I am sure he sees it as a kind of homecoming.

It was also there, in 1990 at the English Open, that Sam typified everything he is about as a golfer and person. I started the last round with a two-shot lead over him and he in turn was two shots clear of the next. It was not one of our better days, and after chopping it around for eleven holes we had slipped back into the pack. I was enjoying a period of depression about the situation. We were walking up the twelfth and Sam said to me, 'Come on, Jesse. Anything can still happen here and one of us can still win it, so let's get stuck in and see what happens.' I am sure Sam's words helped me, and it was a typically wonderful gesture. Four holes later I holed from 40 feet on the last, and Sam followed me in from half the distance to force a play-off which I managed to win at the first extra hole. I do not think Sam would have been much more pleased had he won himself, and it was another superb example of the spirit that exists on the European Tour. Players are genuinely pleased for others when they do win, and it is a quality which will never disappear. We are always willing to help one another, whether it is on the range or through advice over dinner.

Unfortunately, because of what happened at Brookline, particularly on the final day, Sam has not inherited the best of atmospheres, although I am sure he will generate the same spirit and enthusiasm within our next team as was evident throughout the week in Boston. Sam is a fairly relaxed person and takes everything in his stride, and that is a big advantage. He knows the players well too, and mixes with them. What is more, he commands their respect. Basically, it should be easy for him because he has been there, seen it and done it, and he knows exactly what to do.

His ability to be unfazed will also serve him well. It's a quality he displayed one year in Sweden when an almost unbelievable situation with a female marshal distracted him. Having teed his ball close to the right-hand marker, he was just about to take the club back when the woman, standing no more than three or four feet away, started waving her QUIET PLEASE sign in front of his nose. Sam had not yet reached the point of no return and managed to check himself, politely asking the marshal what she was doing. 'It's OK,' she said. 'I am waving to my husband. He has my sandwiches.' Some players might have been tempted to tell the woman her fortune, but Sam waved it off. Knowing him, he probably gave her a ball at the end of the round.

It takes more than a few baps to upset Sam, and anyway, what happens at the Belfry will not initially be down to him at all. The initiative for getting the Ryder Cup back on course will have to come from the Americans. If they believe there was nothing wrong at Brookline they will not be shifting their backsides to put it right. The European supporters know what went on there. They were there, and a lot of them will be at the next one too, and may well be planning to let the Americans have a taste of their own medicine. Our crowd's attitude will probably be determined by the American response; if they do not recognise there was anything wrong, then why should our supporters treat them any different?

I do not want to see the Ryder Cup becoming a match where home advantage is almost decisive because of the crowds, but that appears to be what the Americans went looking for in Boston. I can see the time coming when our players do not want to play in the away match. It is a great occasion, but players will not want to push themselves through too much unpleasantness for the sake of one more Ryder Cup. Aggravation is something we can all do without.

Sam can help, but unless people like the USA's new captain, Curtis Strange, and some of his players think there was a problem, then in their eyes there will be no need to say or do anything. Everyone knows what over-exuberance is – we do see it now and again – but what we saw at Brookline was nothing to do with over-exuberance and everything to do with crowd incitement. Of course you can get excited and go over the top. I remember Tiger Woods going a bit too far when he holed a chip in the Memorial at Muirfield Village, but that was not crowd incitement and Tiger's behaviour at Brookline was exemplary. Some of the other players could learn from him, even though they have been around ten times longer. There is absolutely no place for incitement anywhere in the game of golf

It is a shame, but I fear there is every chance at the Belfry of there being a backlash against the Americans. Our crowds know what went on; they saw it either first-hand or on television, or they read about it in the newspapers. It is not lies, it happened. If the Americans deny it and believe the crowd was OK, if I was a European supporter then I would be inclined to give them a bit back.

I would hate to think the matter would not have been resolved by the time the match returns to the Belfry, but I am sure Sam will have things under control. There were no other candidates to oppose his appointment for the 2001 match, and it might be more difficult to find a successor when Europe returns to the USA in 2003. One assistant, Ian Woosnam, has already been named, and Woosie will have no problems in that role, although I believe he will have every chance of making the team next time, as will Bernhard Langer, who still has an enormous appetite for the game and wants success as much as ever. Woosie has far more in him than I think he appreciates, but if he is confined to a non-playing role he will still be an influence. He is good fun, a strong motivator and an in-your-face fighting Welshman.

Woosie would have been appalled at what happened at Brookline, as would one of the great custodians of the game's traditions. Bobby Jones, the father of the Masters, wrote on the back of Augusta tickets: 'Applauding mistakes is no part of the game of golf, and we hope visitors to the Masters will henceforth observe the etiquette and retain their reputation as among the most knowledgeable and courteous of golfing spectators. The rewards of golf and life too, I suspect, are worth very little unless you play the game by the etiquette as well as the rules.' That philosophy is one which should be shared by all golfers. Similar sentiments, I believe, should be written on the back of Ryder Cup tickets, for I am sure Bobby Jones and Sam Ryder were turning in their graves at what happened on that black Sunday in Boston.

But after all is said and done, it was an experience I would not have missed for the world. It was immensely enjoyable for the most part and I felt my team emerged with great honour from what turned into a very difficult situation. They were the ones upholding the spirit of our sport, one which must be jealously guarded and protected for all those who have gone before us and those who will follow in the future.

12 Me Jane

I WILL NEVER FORGET MARK'S WORDS as we sat on the plane on the way back from Germany and one of the longest weeks of our lives. 'Thank you for coming this week,' he said, words which may seem nothing out of the ordinary, but for me they proved just how traumatic, heart-searching and emotional a time it had been. It was not so much the words he used, but the fact that in all our years together, travelling around the world, it was the first time he had ever said anything remotely like it.

Mark was absolutely shattered, and for once I think he was pleased to have the extra moral support. Minutes before, he had had a second meeting that day with Robert Karlsson, as the friendly Swede tried to come to terms with the fact that he had been overlooked as one of the team's two wild cards. I have never seen Mark so upset as when he had to tell Robert there was no place for him. He was absolutely devastated and totally drained after what a few weeks earlier had looked like being one of the easier jobs of his captaincy went totally pear-shaped.

Standing waiting to board the flight home, someone – Sam, I think – jokingly remarked that all this would be easier next time around. 'No way,' was Mark's reply. 'I never want to do this again, not to friends.' It was very much tongue-in-cheek when I said later that I would divorce Mark if he ever considered being captain again, an easy joke to make when you know you are on solid ground. However, had he been aware of quite how he would feel in Germany, I am not totally convinced he would have accepted the job in the first place. What possibly made an already difficult job for any Ryder Cup captain even harder is the fact that he is still playing full-time on the tour and is therefore living with these guys week in, week out. They are, first and foremost, his friends. The Ryder Cup is an important tournament, but is it that important?

Although Mark was, by the beginning of the 1999 season, well entrenched in his role as captain of the European team, I was still desperate for him to play his way into his own team. I was bitterly disappointed at the Open, when a poor last round scuppered his chances of a high finish and precious Ryder Cup points, and missing the cut in the European Open at the K-Club upset me, which was extremely unusual, because I have always been fairly philosophical about his performances. If he does badly, he does badly, and we get over it and move on, but this time the pressure was even making me tense.

I admit to being frightened to death of doing the job to the extent that, at first, I actually found it quite difficult to talk about it, even to close friends on tour whom I knew would understand, like Beverley Clark, Howard's wife, and Suzanne Torrance. I am sure Beverley must have thought I had gone completely loopy, but I just could not bring myself to discuss it. I am not quite the confident person people perceive me to be. I am a huge worrier, and being part of the team just as a player was really what I wanted Mark to be. In fact, if I am honest, that is what I would have preferred at the time by a million miles, and I held on to that hope throughout a long season.

Before Mark accepted the captaincy, I had always felt the captain was a little bit separate from the rest of the party, and if he had to keep some distance between himself and the players, then would I have to do the same between myself and their wives and partners? Neither of us fits easily into that kind of scenario. Thankfully, that was most definitely not the case, and for 95 per cent of our time in Boston we had an absolute ball. Unfortunately, the memories of that other 5 per cent are just as vivid, and included some which were disgusting and degrading to the perpetrators of the acts which tainted this Ryder Cup.

Until that infamous final day in Boston, Germany was definitely the low point of the term, but for very different reasons. I felt that Sky television were guilty of overstepping the boundaries of decency when they spotted Mark talking in private to Bernhard Langer and set their cameras rolling. Then to misread the situation so badly and assume that Mark was telling Bernhard he was selected was nothing short of diabolical. There was also the first meeting with Robert, and things were all starting to get on top of both of us. It seemed Mark was only a harbinger of bad tidings. I was desperate to get hold of Andrew Coltart so that he could give somebody some good news for a change. I spent two hours trying to get hold of Andrew on his mobile, then his wife, Emma, at home in London, and then his manager, Chubby Chandler, but all to no avail. This was just a bad news day.

Our good friend Ken Brown was a tower of strength for Mark that week, as he was subsequently in his role as assistant captain. Ken backed Mark all the way, telling him again and again that he was making the right choices. He said that, win or lose, Mark had to make decisions he would not regret come 27 September.

Mark is not normally the type of person who suffers from stress. He tends to take things in his stride, particularly where golf is concerned. He is every bit as approachable after shooting an 86 as he is after a 66. What is done is done, and there is no point losing sleep over something you cannot change. However, I think the whole captaincy was more stressful than he would admit, and I remain convinced that the week spent agonising over his two wild cards, not to mention missing out on making the team himself, caused the attack of shingles which followed the BMW International at Munich.

Thankfully, Mark recovered fairly quickly, and now that we finally knew that he was definitely going to be captain rather than a player, we both threw ourselves into making as good a job as possible. We would only be doing it once, so we might as well do it right. All I tried to do with the girls was exactly what Mark did with the boys: I wanted them to know that I was always available, that if there was anything they wanted to know or were unsure about, then all they had to do was ask. I wanted nothing to detract from the team spirit, and I do not think anything did. We arrived friends and left, if anything, even bigger friends. Dawn Brown and Suzanne Torrance, the wives of Mark's assistant captains, Ken and Sam, were absolutely brilliant. Neither of us could have asked for better, and from my side it was a case of opposites attract. Suzanne is so hyper, and being an actress is not what she does, it is just who she is. She has a talent for making anyone feel special, and boy, can she party! Dawn is a completely different personality to Suzanne, quiet yet very reassuring, and there were several times during the week I was extremely grateful to have her there. I tend to fall somewhere in the middle. It seemed to make a pretty good mix.

Most of the player's partners were known to me, but I had not previously met Marian Lawrie or Brigitte Van de Velde. Jarmo Sandelin's partner, Linda, was in a bit of a quandary over whether she should assume her usual role as caddie, or hand over the bag to someone else and join us mere 'spectators' for the week. In the end, she chose the latter, which was certainly a popular decision as far as I was concerned. Both she and Jarmo were fantastic company all week. I do not think I ever saw either of them without a grin from ear to ear. Monserrat Jiménez and I had communicated by sign language only over the years. Her English and my Spanish are pretty much of the same standard: non-existent. Fortunately, Sergio's lovely mum, Consuela, was with us for the week, which I am sure made the ladies' outings and lunches much more enjoyable for Monserrat. My only regret so far as the ladies were concerned is that Emma Coltart was unable to join us due to having just given birth to Bonnie. However, we kept in touch by phone and she was a great support to me during the weeks leading up to the tournament – amazingly so really, considering this was Andrew's first Ryder Cup.

One of the few possibly contentious decisions I had to take was about team garb for the girls at the opening and closing ceremonies. I have always been dead against it. The players are the team, they have worked bloody hard to earn the privilege of wearing a uniform, and I am afraid I was unwilling even to discuss that particular issue. However, on-course clothing was a slightly different matter. Even though it would not be my choice for us to be kitted out in matching gear, I can appreciate why some people might be in favour of it. The public like it because they can immediately pick out Darren's wife or Paul's wife or whoever from the other fifty 'hangers-on' inside the ropes (do not get me going on that one!). One or two of the girls would have liked it because 'we wouldn't have to worry about what to wear'. It certainly saves showing your credentials every two minutes in order to gain access to wherever you need to go.

To this end, I did try very hard, along with Escada in Munich, to put together a uniform for the three match days. Katja and Lulu at Escada were extremely helpful, but in all honesty, it just was not coming together. We were twelve women ranging, in age, from 21 to 40(ish), from my height, five feet ten inches, to Laurae Westwood's five nothing, with different builds, different colouring and even different nationalities, which in Europe does make a difference when buying clothes – absolutely impossible. Once the decision was taken to abandon our efforts, I have to admit to feeling mightily relieved. Personally, if I am going to be criticised for my dress sense and be compared to the Americans, I would rather it be for something of my own choosing. It would not be the first time I was hoist with my own petard, and almost certainly will not be the last!

Although the uniform debate did cause a bit of an issue, it did not, to my knowledge, create any bad feeling. The atmosphere in the team room was wonderful. This in itself is not quite as easy to achieve as you may think. Some people need a bit of cajoling, some just get stuck in and enjoy themselves, others need leaving alone and find their own way in the end. It's nearly back to the uniform issue: you cannot expect everyone to be alike.

In fact, we had a really good time, and the only problems throughout the week were one or two small hangovers. The wives and partners of both teams, and those of the tournament officials, were treated to a tour of Boston, Harvard in particular, followed by lunch at the Harvard Boat House. Mrs Barbara Bush was the speaker on Tuesday, and I must say she seemed a very warm and genuine person, who works tirelessly for various charities. She was not, however, afraid to let everybody know where her loyalties lay come Friday morning.

On Wednesday we ate together again, this time lunch in the Four Seasons hotel, where the flower displays on the tables were by far the most spectacular I have ever seen in my life. This was a reasonably short affair, as Wednesday evening is traditionally the gala dinner. This year we were entertained by the brilliant Boston Pops, followed by Celine Dion, who was out of this world. None of our team could quite believe it when Ben had us all marched off home to bed at ten o'clock! Still, at least none of our party fell asleep this time, unlike someone fairly high up in the scheme of things, who fell asleep while Johnny Mathis was singing in 1995!

Ben and Julie Crenshaw must have worked extremely hard to bring all this together, so it was a great pity that everything was overshadowed by the controversy which surrounded the matches, particularly on the final day. If I felt for anybody, it was definitely Eimear Montgomerie and what she must have had to put up with when the galleries turned on Monty. However, she remained so cool, calm and collected that I never felt she needed looking after. She never once complained – publicly, anyway.

The first inkling I had that there had been any trouble at all was when I heard Julie Crenshaw and some of the other American girls apologising profusely to her in the ladies' loo during the rain delay on Saturday – this while we were all drying each other's hair, bottoms and other areas with as many hair dryers as the golf club could muster.

I have walked round golf courses for years listening to people saying what a 'miserable bastard' Mark is, what a dreadful walk he has got, how many caddies he gets through because they cannot stand to caddy for him (I think I can recall five in twenty years). I usually let them dig themselves into a big deep hole before introducing myself and pointing out that Mark actually speaks very highly of them and perhaps they might care to reconsider their judgement. Having heard what was said to and about Monty, I have cringed at my reaction to criticism of Mark, because it is obviously nothing compared to what Eimear goes through whenever she is in the USA. It is much harder to listen to hurtful comments about somebody you love than to hear them made about yourself. Monty must be very conscious that it is worse for Eimear than it is for him.

To a certain extent, when somebody becomes at all famous, let alone as famous as Monty, they become public property. Although this is unavoidable – indeed, it goes with the territory – why should that entitle complete strangers to hurl insults at him? Would you walk up to a complete stranger in the street and say, 'My God, aren't you fat/thin/ugly/boring'? Unfortunately, I am not as cool as Eimear. I find it very difficult to keep my mouth shut.

We had very mixed reports from friends and family about spectator behaviour during the week. Without exception, they all seemed thoroughly to enjoy the experience. Unfortunately, however, there were also some quite nasty moments. For instance, one friend of ours, on being 'exposed' as hailing from England, was asked, quite violently, why she 'didn't get the f*** out of Ireland'. Our parents and other close family members found it quite hard going in the clubhouse on occasions. Being outnumbered at such close quarters by so many of the USA team's nearest and dearest was, I think, much more daunting an experience than they had anticipated, and my family are hardened rugby fans. Nobody expected the USA team's family and friends to cheer Europe on, but their 'win at all costs' attitude can be very hard to take.

It must be said, though, that not everyone in the gallery was hostile towards us. There were equally as many fans there who were welcoming, very friendly and who seemed genuinely embarrassed by the behaviour of the few thugs who were doing their best to spoil it for us all.

Meanwhile, back in the team room, we were still having a great time. In all the Ryder Cups I have been to as part of the team, I have never before seen everyone sitting glued to the television to watch the mandatory press conferences being broadcast live, let alone delay departure back to the hotel in order not to miss the end of one. In fact, I think the American media were so taken with our boys that they appeared to have deserted their own men. As a result, I think the USA team, their wives, officials, ex-captains et al, were urged to get everyone back on side. Only an opinion, but that is how it appeared to me.

There was the odd incident on the golf course during Friday and Saturday, which should really have been a warning of what was to come on Sunday. For instance, I literally bumped into one of the player's wives as she was yelling 'Crush 'em!' at the top of her voice, while waving her fist manically. She apologised immediately, saying, 'I didn't see you there.' When I asked her what difference that made, she did not really have an answer. Marian Lawrie stood next to another of their girls who was urging Paul's ball into the water before he had even taken a practice swing. Can you imagine having lunch and dinner for two days with friends who are now standing beside you vehemently wishing you ill?

It is extremely difficult to write about the final day without sounding like a 'sore loser', but I find it impossible to accept the way some of them behaved. I am not a particularly competitive person (the only thing I ever won in my life was the school music festival), but I am always up for a celebration, whoever the victor. In fact, when we lost the Ryder Cup at Kiawah Island in 1991, Mark and Bernard Gallacher came looking for me when I was still on the green congratulating the USA team on their victory. This time, however, it was very different. When I met Julie Crenshaw on the eighteenth green that day, I found it difficult to say anything. There was no doubt that their team had played brilliant golf all day, it was a great comeback for them and under almost any other circum-stances it would have been easy to say 'Well played, see you in two years' time.' However, the way they carried on on the golf course that final day left a very bitter taste and spoiled what had been a great week.

The media seemed primarily concerned with the infamous seventeenth green incident during Olly's singles match. To be honest, this was not the worst of it all for me. The Americans had about forty cheer-leaders inside the ropes with every match, all whooping up the crowd, gesturing to them to make more noise, be more aggressive. Even the players themselves were at it. Never mind whether they were standing right next to one of us, it was the most discourteous display I have ever witnessed, on or off a golf course, and I cannot describe how insulted I felt. All the other European wives were feeling exactly the same, and it was quite hard to dissuade one or two of them from retaliating. Poor Laurae Westwood was nearly beside herself, and although I could very easily have got stuck in with her, why bring ourselves down to their level? So we just tried to keep smiling. I kept telling her what my mum always tells me: 'Kill 'em with kindness.'

So, back to the seventeenth. Although the incident was unfortunate and distressing, it was more forgivable than the rest of the day's behaviour. The Americans thought they had won already, so I put what happened there down to natural exuberance, which I totally understand. I do think, though, that when realisation dawned, Justin Leonard might have picked Olly's ball up and moved on to the eighteenth tee, but that was never going to happen.

The Brookline Ryder Cup seems to have been continually compared to Kiawah in 1991. Well I was at both and I can assure you there is no comparison. At Kiawah, I spent quite a good few holes each day outside the ropes among the crowd. There was definitely banter, but I honestly do not remember anyone being rude or insulting. At Brookline, I am not sure I would have dared walk outside the ropes; it was intimidating enough inside them. The USA team at Kiawah seemed to be under the impression that America had single-handedly won the Gulf War, which many Europeans found a bit galling. Corey Pavin drew particular criticism for waving his Desert Storm hat as though he had actually bombed Saddam himself, but Corey is a great bloke who has since apologised to Mark and me far too often for his behaviour that week. When Corey and Jim Gallagher Jr beat Mark and Costantino Rocca at the Belfry in 1993, Mark and Corey rode back to the clubhouse on the same buggy. Not much chance of that sort of thing happening in Boston.

The closing ceremony could have been difficult, but it was not really. Mark made a great (short) speech which made us chuckle, and not joining in the applause when Ben thanked the Boston crowd made us feel we had made a point, however small. Then it was back for another end-of-Ryder-Cup celebration. I will not pretend that we were all immediately in party mood, but a drop of the fizzy stuff works wonders, and we were shortly to be seen dancing in the compound outside our team room at the side of the clubhouse. We continued in this vein until heaven knows what time on Monday morning. It was a fairly quiet trip home.

There were to be few acknowledgements of wrongdoing at Brookline. Julie Crenshaw was genuinely sorry for what Eimear had had to put up with in particular, and for the crowd's behaviour in general, but, unfortunately, she was completely missing the point. To be honest, I do not think that any one of them can see our point at all. For this reason, it is difficult to see how things can be improved in the future. I am quite sure that, were they to read this book, Ben and his team would respond by saying, 'Well, so and so did this' and 'You said that', and they may well have legitimate points. I am not trying to imply that Europeans are perfect; we all have our moments, especially under pressure. In fact, I am probably more likely than most to fly off the handle, especially in the defence of a close friend or someone I love. But to deliberately set out to rile and intimidate during a tournament like the Ryder Cup is, to my mind, inexcusable.

I do not want this chapter of mine to make it sound as though we do not get on with the American players and their wives. We do. Neither do I want it to sound as though we did not enjoy our time in Boston. We did. I hope that what I have written here will not lose me friends over there. It may well, but I hope not. Ben and Julie have been friends of ours for a long time, as indeed have many other members of their 1999 team, but it can be difficult when someone finds it impossible to see your point of view.

One friend we have most definitely lost is Payne Stewart, who, even if he could not see our point of view, was more than happy to sit and listen to it for long enough during dinner at the Dunhill Cup. His death puts trivial things like golf tournaments into perspective, and we will all miss him.

Following our return from Boston, we received hundreds of letters from all over the world, many even from America, congratulating Mark and his team on their dignified behaviour during all the turmoil of the final round. Their behaviour, and indeed that of their wives and girlfriends, was exemplary, and I am inordinately proud of every one of them. But I will not be doing it again.

Jane James

13 Quote, unquote

'We welcome you in the spirit of what Samuel
Ryder started and I hope that spirit never dies.'
Ben Crenshaw at the opening ceremony

'It's one of the most disgusting things I have seen
in my life. Tom Lehman calls himself a man of god, but
his behaviour has been disgusting today.'
Sam Torrance

'I felt embarrassed for golf. It went way beyond
the decency you associate with proper golf. I love the
Ryder Cup and I don't want to see it degenerate
into a mob demonstration every time we play it.'
Sir Michael Bonallack

'Cheering when you miss putts or hit into bunkers
is one thing. But personal abuse is something different.
We are going to get into a situation where fights
will break out if we don't stop this thing now.'
Mark James

'There was over-exuberance, no question about it.
It wasn't a very good thing, but what's done is done.
Europe had a great party at Valderrama and we
had to watch and now it's their turn.'
Tom Lehman

'I was shocked by it, but I don't think it would have
made a difference.'
Butch Harmon on the seventeenth green incident

'I said I thought we were a better team and that
we should go out and show it. "Let's go and kill them,"
is what I actually said.'
David Duval

'My only comments last night were if we do go
down, let's go down with all our oars in the water.'
Hal Sutton

'As far as the seventeenth green is concerned and
what happened in the Leonard–Olazábal match, we do
apologise sincerely. The celebration spilled over
and it shouldn't have done and for that we
are truly sorry.'
Ben Crenshaw

'I was playing behind José Maria and I couldn't
believe what I saw happen at the seventeenth green. I
felt sure that when the celebrating finished they
would all walk on to the next tee, but then
I saw José Maria standing there on his own trying
to make a putt and I thought, "This is unbelievable".'
Colin Montgomerie

'I don't think these things should happen on a golf course anywhere. You show respect for your opponent.'
José Maria Olazábal

'As far as the heckling I took this week is concerned, well I now use it as a motivating factor and as a compliment because it must mean that I can play this game quite well.'
Colin Montgomerie

'A lot of players will not be bothered about competing in America again. Certainly that is the case with me. It's not something I would look forward to. We don't need to be treated like this.'
Mark James

'I learned over the weekend that Michelob beer is to be the official drink at the next Ryder Cup. To me, that does not make sense. They should be thinking in terms of orange juice.'
Colin Montgomerie

'I cannot tell you the number of occasions I had to back off a shot. Personal attacks should never happen. And it's not just me on the receiving end of them nowadays. Most of the Europeans had a taste of the treatment over the weekend.'
Colin Montgomerie

'Obviously Boston was swept up in emotion. To suggest Europeans are not vocal is wrong. They are. The Ryder Cup is about partisan support. Believe me, it's no different than from when we're over there. Just ask some of the players who played at Valderrama. It's not like this has never happened before.'
Ben Crenshaw

'It's time to sit down and think about what we can do about verbal abuse on the golf course. We're not blaming the result on that. You expect excitement. In Kiawah in 1991 it was "War on the Shore" stuff. It was very partisan and there was a lot of cheering. That wasn't very nice but it reached a whole new level this week with personal insults. None of us think it has any place within the game. We want golf to be kept absolutely clean and we're going to have to think what to do about it.'
Mark James

'Their behaviour was just ridiculous. I don't mind it when we've both played, but to do it before the next opponent hits a shot, then it's just not on. If it means that much to them, then all the best to them.'
Paul Lawrie on supporters calling out

'I'm wondering whether I should step out of the country. Maybe I should cancel my flight to Spain to play in the World Championship at Valderrama in November. If I do go to Spain it will be as though I'll be wearing a bullseye on my back.'
Justin Leonard

'For Justin Leonard to say he is too scared to play on this side of the Atlantic is nonsense. No American will have anything to fear. They won't look for revenge in Scotland. Certainly a Scottish crowd will not react like the American fans. They are far more knowledgeable and know how to appreciate good shots whatever their nationality. The applause might be a bit muted, especially for Lehman, because the Scots like everybody else will have been disappointed by what he did.'
Bernard Gallacher

'I don't condone what went on with the players at the seventeenth green, but I can understand the spontaneous reaction to Leonard's putt by the players.'
Curtis Strange

'I thought it was horrible conduct, there's no question about that. We've got to take those people out of the crowd and out the gate. But I don't think what happened on Sunday represents all the American fans. It was unfortunate but it happens.'
Jim Awtrey, chief executive, US PGA

'If the Ryder Cup has to be like this in the future
then I don't want to play any more Ryder Cups. The
tradition of the Ryder Cup is very important and
it was nice to be there and to be involved,
but what happened in Brookline is not what it is
about. It was like professional ice hockey or football
players rather than professional golfers. I never
spoke to the American players about it, but
to me they are not the winners. That is my point
of view. I feel they didn't deserve it after what
happened on the last day.'
Miguel Angel Jiménez

'The bottom line is that the whole world saw what
happened and the whole world is going to judge what
their behaviour was like. All we ask is respect from
our opponents.'
José Maria Olazábal